LEAVING ANALYSIS

LEAVING ANALYSIS

A YEAR FINDING FREUD, REDISCOVERING THE SACRED

NICOLA MENDENHALL

atmosphere press

Published by Atmosphere Press

ISBN 978-1-63988-658-6

Cover design by Ronaldo Alves

atmospherepress.com

For Wendell

CONTENTS

NOTE TO READER EXPLAINING CHAPTER TITLES & FREE ASSOCIATION

I am indebted to Shaman John Broomfield, a friend since 1994, for calling my attention to the prolific writings of John Matthews and for issuing an invitation to an Advanced Shamanic workshop that I reference in the Prologue.

My consequent reading of *The Celtic Shaman: A Handbook* (1991), by John Matthews, introduced Shamanism as a way of working with the self, which called to my mind Sigmund Freud's creation of psychoanalysis, where the analytic attitude is used in service of developing self-knowledge. Matthews writes that shamans must learn to know and recognize their inner self and suggests there are twelve stages on the shaman's journey. When my eyes read the words describing the steps shamans traverse for self-discovery, goose bumps rose up and down my arms and legs.

Encountering this list of surprisingly familiar words gave me a precise way of describing the termination process I was outlining in my second memoir. These twelve words (that I use as chapter titles) embodied the essence of the yearlong termination process from Freudian Psychoanalysis, an analytical journey that lasted fourteen years. I am grateful to John Matthews for his clear representation of the natural progression of transformation.

On the psychoanalytic couch, I learned to let go of knowing what was going to come out of my mouth and trust that my unconscious would feed me what I needed. In psychoanalysis, this is known as free association, and the habit of thinking this way may be evident in my story as you read further. I have attempted to make my associations clear, but at times you may need to call upon your unconscious to make the connections you desire.

PROLOGUE

My mind begged for immersion in the now, my body flooded with sensory stimulus as my feet stepped off the path, a well-worn path that meandered through the forest encircling Wangapeka Retreat Centre. Soaking up the music of silence, I slowly made my way to the edge of a circle of trees where people have gathered since the beginning of time. Once there, I surrendered to the felt sense of spirit, an experience I later discovered psychoanalysts know as non-psychotic magic.

A feeling of deliberateness and spaciousness, similar to that cultivated by meditation, began to settle in my body as I sat on a felled tree and focused my attention on the space I inhabited. Reminded of minutes spent at home on my sturdy wooden meditation bench, time expanded and contracted. Something was happening. I felt a sense of being. This experience transpired in December 2018, after my oldest son and I braved the seventeen-hour flight from Iowa to New Zealand.

Today, when I slow down, stop searching or striving, close my eyes, I can picture how in New Zealand the light filtered through the trees. I can feel the air on my skin, hear my warm heart finding its own rhythm, remember the deep, easy breathing that calmed my psyche. To breathe so easily was paradoxical because at that time I simultaneously wanted to stay forever—the silence felt sacred—and depart—because my intuition discerned I needed this new way of being and that it would be restorative in my regular life.

Much time would pass before I comprehended the transformational significance of those moments of silent awe and how they were leading me toward a new juxtaposition between the secular and the sacred. Time before I would begin to take myself seriously and develop a sense of agency that knew my unitary nature could now integrate unconscious, preconscious, and conscious states.

This new sense of agency would replace my omnipotence, which the analyst had described as a non-reality-based need for control. Time to wrestle with questions about getting old and getting sick and accept, welcome, and celebrate my multifaceted spiritual nature. Time to claim the freedom of expression that would allow me to explore the person I was and find new parts in my brain and mind. Time before I would permanently release the four-sessions a week psychoanalytic treatment where I could speak whatever was on my mind, be silent when there was nothing I wanted to say, tell stories about other people in my life without fear of reprisal, admit cruelties, challenge, weep, or be with my inner self. Accompanying me was an analyst who midwifed my awakening. During the termination year that I will be describing in these chapters, I discarded the fantasy that she was godlike and all-knowing. And finally, gave up the wish she would be a new best friend or colleague.

More time would pass as I comprehended the depth that psychoanalysis offered me as a method of investigation, a mode of treatment, and a theory of human development; time before I understood more clearly the psychoanalytic principles that had begun to heal me. Time to decide I wanted to be a serious student of Freud's biography, discovering reasons a considerable number of people were obsessed with him even today; how important it was for me to know him as a person and compare the society he lived in with mine of the twenty-first century and research thoroughly what Freud thought about religion. Time to know the beauty and feelings that can be experienced in the art world related to the basic necessity of humans to express themselves. Time to discover the common threads of how I make meaning of The Inner Life using philosophy, religion, meditation, mysticism, metaphysics, psychology. Time to explore the relationship between the mind and body. Time to acknowledge that the approaching termination not only was filled with losses but sparked new beginnings. Time to realize that what I was searching for outside of me, was inside me. Time to recognize and nurture an urgency to begin creating a new narrative for this life-changing integration.

I had strategically separated my spiritual essence from my sophisticated life in analysis to manage what I saw as disparate parts of myself. I was blind to this split in my psyche, encouraged by the self-imposed separation between analysis and the sacred something. The psyche does not like to feel split. This split occurred in a parallel way to how, as a child, I had ignored the separation that occurred between my mother and me when my siblings were born.

In both of these life-changing situations, psychoanalytic treatment and my siblings' births, I had acted as if nothing had changed, enjoying the protection of denial. I had yet to learn the wisdom of ambivalence and the joy of integration. Psychoanalysis was designed to change me, yet I remained largely landlocked in my crafted oldest child persona, hunkered down behind damning defenses that prevented their detection by others as well as myself. This remained truer than I discerned, I am loath to say, after more than a decade of psychoanalytic sessions. Distracted and misled by superficial emotions, mistaking avoidance for action, quiet for peace, failing to open to metaphoric meaning and largely unaware of all my contradictions, denials, and defenses, I remained, in many ways, unchanged, unaware of the unconscious, stuck in my above it all persona. Afraid to transform.

In the year of termination, I discovered it was time to relinquish acting irresponsibly, currying confusion, and resisting the claim I did not know enough to speak about Freud's creation of psychoanalysis or find my own voice. These strategies were familiar, and I was reluctant to abandon the safety they provided, but I knew it was time.

In my mind, analysis had pointed me toward and endorsed a secular way of life. I had ignored my heart and soul, both of which yearned for the world of the sacred that I had ignored. On one hand, to let go of psychoanalysis was admitting there was no single answer to my question about living life to the fullest, but on the other, letting go was acknowledgement that creating my own path of integration was the next necessary step on the journey.

When I learned that Freud was slow to realize the Nazi threat in Vienna and did not think he and his family needed to leave Austria for their safety, it was a shocking blow to my omniscient stance that Freud was the person I could trust wholeheartedly to know the right way to stay safe. I promised myself, as I prepared to leave the safety of analysis—which had itself unbeknownst to me become a state of partial lockdown—that I would not jump into a way of life that included all my mistaken notions from before analysis but that I would continue the painstaking work of study, contemplation, and integration.

When I entered treatment, you could say that I was a seeker of magic, looking for one person or theory to trust, wanting to believe that psychoanalysis or the analyst would have all the answers, would satisfy my need to know. Now this seeker of magic became a container for insight. I discovered as the termination year unfolded, I wanted magic that did not deny reality. Magic that Freud approved of and recognized. Little did I know that the ending of psychoanalytic treatment would, in reality, be more of a beginning than an ending.

I

FIRST REALIZATION

November 2019

One result of extensive, insightful, transformative Freudian analysis was the discovery of an underlying conflict buried deep in my unconscious. This struggle between the desire to cling to the familiar while yearning for exotic ways of being in the world was a predominantly psychological dilemma and, as such, begged for psychoanalytic scrutiny. Asking myself if I was a godless secularist residing in the present age or a seeker of ageless spiritual mysticism could bring on a feeling of panic. What made this question so perilous? The answer is another question for which I have no answer, only speculation. If I remain wedded to the version of Sigmund Freud that insists he distrusted religion, finding meaning in my life might be, dare I say, impossible? On the other hand, if I grasp the sacred as a presence in the world, will I be deluded? This question revolves around finding meaning in life.

As November—the first month of my termination year—

launched, I could sometimes feel how the paradoxical puzzle of the familiar or the exotic was lessening. The analyst and I had explored my relationship history with the bulk of the evidence indicating that it was rarely me who severed friend, family, or professional connections. Yet I had taken a giant step forward and initiated the termination process, which would entail the dissolution of a bond without precedent. Previously, I had clung to connections with a fierceness worthy of a warrior, warrior being a word Buddhists use to describe persons who fearlessly follow the spiritual path. Granted, I had proposed an entire calendar year to execute this separation—but I was preparing to let go of this analytic relationship that had been like no other, which had literally changed my life. And not to sound too dramatic, but I believe the relationship saved my life or at least spared me excess anxiety and multiple physical symptoms.

Connections with sentient beings were only the beginning of my struggle of letting go. When the analyst, Denae, became accredited with an organization that included the word Christian in its title, I felt betrayed. Wasn't she Freudian and didn't that mean that she was godless like I had heard Freud was and where I was perhaps headed? I thought I had settled the question of Christianity in that I didn't believe in a God outside of myself any longer. But her professional accreditation brought up once again my dilemma of whether or not to give up on the Christian God, a god I had worshipped faithfully but had begun to loathe when my feminist consciousness grew and I noted that god continued, for the most part, to be a 'him.'

This talk of pronouns brings to mind an English teacher employed by my son's high school who purposefully didn't own a car and, before it was in fashion, walked everywhere for environmental reasons. In the 1980s, she invited me to meditate with her Zen group. She was single and appeared to be more sophisticated than my United Methodist friends.

Accompanying her to zazen, the Zen name for meditating, was my first encounter with robed priests and monotonically chanting the heart sutra. I had been impressed with the seriousness I witnessed. There was no small talk.

I was enchanted with what appeared to me, a young married mother of three, the English teacher's monastic lifestyle. Previously, when I had investigated Buddhism, I pegged it as a philosophy, not a religion, but this ritual display moved me deeply. Nonetheless, I continued to stubbornly separate Buddhism from spirituality for many years.

When I heard that Buddha warned against grasping, I could feel the familiar paradoxical inner tension surfacing. I was not one to let go of relationships or lifestyles; grasping the familiar had ensured my security. My reluctance to relinquish the bonds I cherished with others made it tough to tune into and finally admit that my time in analysis was, in fact, nearing an end. During a mid-October 2019 session, I reluctantly articulated this to the analyst:

"I am thinking it is time to discontinue my analytical process."

Hearing my trembling voice, the analyst did not make any reassuring sounds but simply offered this response: "There are two questions to consider if you wish to discuss termination."

She paused. I couldn't see her from my supine position on the couch, but I heard her take a breath. "First, you would need to determine if you really want to terminate."

My inner impatience roiled dangerously close to the surface. I screamed internally to myself, *wasn't that what I just said?* Thankfully, I had grown too mature to stomp my feet in toddler mode; still, I was struggling with feelings I wished weren't there. Was I really ready to stop coming? Yes, I felt certain that I was. My response, I hoped, contained minimal brusqueness: "I said I am ready to stop analysis." I still didn't want to upset her.

The analyst did not acknowledge any rudeness on my part, choosing to remain neutral as classical theory dictates. After a several-minute pause, she calmly expressed the second question: "How long do you want the termination process to last?"

At this juncture, I flashed on my habitual pattern of wanting things settled and decided, which still occupied top priority as my default position. This was a position I desperately wanted to cling to; though the satisfaction of having the decision made in this case was tempting, as in I could give her an answer right then, I remembered how often this rapid way of making decisions had backfired in the past and not produced the results I had desired. Using the attitude she and I formerly referred to as being above it all, I began thinking silently about her second question. How soon could I wrap things up? Would a month be enough time to go through fond farewells? Musing on how awkward it might be to attend sessions for a whole month with the knowledge that I was already finished, my anxiety ramped up. What on earth would we talk about for all that time? Maybe two weeks would be more appropriate? Would that be enough time?

Evidently, I had learned a fair amount during my couch time because I did not ask about a month, let alone two weeks, but instead, proceeded to act as I felt a credible analyzed woman would act. Though I was ready to terminate, I informed her I would need time to decide on the length of the termination process.

Taking my time driving home that day, I pondered this second question and distracted myself by worrying about how much I disliked the word termination. It sounded like death. So final. Sometimes I found myself free-associating like this when I felt the anxiety I continued to experience more often than I wished. I reluctantly conceded that termination was the psychoanalytic word used for ending treatment, so I best get used to it. Enamored of most everything else about psychoanalysis, a decision was made to tolerate the word. You may note a trace of omnipotence here, but at that time, I didn't.

When I turned the corner onto my street, another question occurred to me: who in their right mind would give up the opportunity to consult with a professionally trained experienced analyst, a person who happened to be a veritable treasure chest of knowledge about their patient's inner workings? And in this case, an analyst who not only knew me, but knew my husband, my siblings, my friends—none of whom she had, of course, ever met in person. My assessment was that she knew all of their inner workings more intimately than I, even though she only knew them through my particular lens—an example of how I periodically granted her magical powers.

The truth was, I reminded myself as I continued my reverie, I was related to these humans in ways she was not, and I had known them much longer. However, her memory of things from my past, secrets I had confided in her and then never mentioned again, sometimes because I forgot and sometimes because they were too embarrassing to repeat, was bewildering. Her recall was incredibly accurate, and she inserted the details at exactly the right moment to make a point that was normally hard to refute. She deduced when I harbored anger towards her. I knew this because she skillfully incorporated my resentments in her clever interpretations.

I then pulled my car into the garage, entered through the kitchen, and made my way to the living room where I plopped down on my comfortable reading chair and closed my eyes with the intention of contemplating the analyst's second question: How long did I want the termination process to be? Instinctively, I began practicing the breathing technique of inhaling to the count of four, holding for the count of four, then exhaling for the count of four. I was barely through two rounds of the breath cycle when information came from somewhere. Was it a thought? An intuition? A message from my guides, as some of my spiritual friends would say? Regardless of its origination, the message was crystal clear: One year.

I pulled the pure green wool throw tighter around me and marveled: A year? I bet nobody takes an entire year to leave analysis. I stopped myself from employing my father's word ridiculous, although taking an entire year to terminate did seem to merit the use of his word. But then I considered my deepest yearning, though still quite hazy. I've always been a seeker, was all I could articulate. Perhaps this was the rationale behind the lengthy termination period. I wasn't sure, but I continued to listen. Then, I began to bargain with the mysterious pronouncement that had seemingly come from nowhere and I asked: "How about six months?" There was a beat of silence before the initial message was repeated: One year.

Okay, I thought, sitting there in my reading chair in my living room. I asked and the message I received was clear. One year. It had been crystal clear. My secular side wanted to distrust the answer, but I remembered how the message had felt in my body. The information had sunk down into my belly, leaving me in a restful state, feeling embraced by my reading chair. Now, I thought to myself, all that remains is telling the analyst I need one year to terminate, and I can do that the next session.

I continued to rest in my comfortable chair peacefully while thinking about psychoanalysis. I wondered if I had learned all that I could learn from Freud's creation. At each juncture in my treatment, when I thought I was ready to end the process, at the next session, we burrowed down to another level in my psyche and discovered an entirely new view of my dysfunctional patterns that it felt vital to my continued well-being to explore. I wanted to learn everything possible. I wanted it all! Several years ago an astrologer informed me that my ascendent Virgo meant I was always focused on getting better at what I was doing. It felt doubtful to me that I had discovered everything lurking in my unconscious, but I hoped it was true I had discovered enough about myself that I could manage the rest of my life while coping with ordinary unhappiness.

Ordinary unhappiness was the phrase Freud coined to describe the desired results of psychoanalysis, a phrase that sounded pessimistic to me at the beginning of treatment. Toward the end of my sessions, the phrase had evolved in my mind to feel more optimistic. Now that I knew ordinary unhappiness was common and, in some ways, though it seemed weird to say, a desired state, I no longer blamed myself when not totally happy. The result was that when I didn't feel content, it didn't feel as bad. I would say to myself, *here it is again, ordinary unhappiness*. But could I really manage ordinary unhappiness all by myself? Winding down my ruminations, I rose from my chair to go for my walk and wait for my next session so I could get this all settled. I love having things decided.

On October 30, 2019, during our regular analytical session, I informed the analyst I needed a year to complete the termination process. I said that each month of the next year would be the last month I would ever be in psychoanalysis. Of course, the analyst's response didn't provide a clue as to whether she approved or disapproved. She was a psychoanalyst. She accepted my decision, didn't ask any questions. Didn't give me approval or disapproval. We just went on with the session. The last year of analysis would begin on Friday, November 1, 2019.

Thankfully, the waiting period for November 1, a day that would commemorate the joyous advent of the termination process of psychoanalytic treatment, wasn't very lengthy. I was disconcerted that occasional doubts crept into my mind, first cousins to fears of water and mice that I had been trying to slough off years ago when I began psychoanalysis. In my usual fashion of finding reasons to be hard on myself, I bemoaned the fact I was no longer attending water aerobics classes, but then reminded myself with a newly developed supportive self that I had tentatively begun to loosen my two-handed grip on the side of the pool before I stopped going to class. I uncharacteristically cheered myself on: a loosened grip must count for something. I now appreciated the healing properties of water, knew its restorative and refreshing qualities. I would never swim the English Channel, but since that wasn't on my bucket list, I was going to count my appreciation for water as a success.

I then contemplated how the analyst never gave up on me. Week after week, month after month, year after year. She gave me the impression, albeit without words, that it was important to her I continued in treatment. When I was thinking clearly, she affirmed me by offering a hum of agreement, and when I was stuttering and confused, she stayed present, silently celebrating with me for finally expressing emotions, then waited with me while I got myself together. She was a true professional who knew I wanted to know the unvarnished truth about my emotional experience and supplied me with just the right amount of support to keep me motivated but not overwhelmed.

Because I was a stubborn person and a tough client—I knew this from my own experience as a psychotherapist working with certain clients, clients that unfortunately were a lot like me—I also knew that I probably appeared obnoxious to her. I knew that I could be a pain in the neck. I remembered the days when, as a therapist, I had ushered a client into my office, hoping and praying they would have made progress. That they would not continue to challenge me on every suggestion I offered or question every observation I shared. I'm sure at the time I didn't remember that I had the tendency to do both of those things in response to my analyst's complex, sophisticated interpretations. I believed that seeing therapy from both sides of the couch was advantageous for me as a therapist and as a client.

The big day, Friday, November 1, 2019, arrived. On this momentous day, my feet toasty in Ugg boots crossed the threshold of the psychoanalyst's office. This first day of the last November, I would meet with my analyst, a woman who had become an integral part of my inner and outer, personal and professional, real and imagined life over the course of ten years. Complex, meaningful, multilayered, at times baffling psychoanalytic conversations had become a staple for me, feeling as essential as swallowing the supplements prescribed by my nurse practitioner. Now that there was an end in sight, my deepest desire to learn all that I could took on an urgency that surprised me.

For the first few minutes of the session, the silence felt comfortable. I was lying on the couch. I utilized some of the precious minutes of this session to reaffirm to myself and to the analyst that I was indeed ready to terminate, mindfully using the preferred word for closure so as to appear sophisticated and technically correct. I affirmed clearly and resolutely once more to myself and the analyst that I wanted the termination process to happen over the course of one year. Since I was lying on the couch, I could not see her expression. Was she surprised at my need to affirm this again?

Suddenly, I needed to go to the restroom. I paid attention to this bodily sensation, which had been a continuing challenge since my 2016 diagnosis of Normal Pressure Hydrocephalus. One of NPH's symptoms was incontinence. Sometimes, even when, for the most part I no longer had incontinence, I misread the signals or waited too long and had accidents. Accidents that felt humiliating and very Freudian in nature. I did not like to talk to anyone about this issue, not even the analyst.

When I came back from the restroom, having made it in time, which left me with a feeling of confidence, I easily resumed my supine posture. Even though I knew I had just spoken of my termination plans, the new sense of self I felt compelled me to ask: "Are you with me on the termination plan?"

"Why did you ask me then?" was her response.

"My mind brought it up," was my chilly defensive answer.

"You were asking your mind?" From then on in the session, I was confused and anxious. Thankfully I took good journal notes, because I have no memory of an exchange where I said, "I got tired of swimming in the pool" but it is recorded clearly, and my assumption now is that I was referring to the dream I had months ago where I was needing help to stay afloat. Her response was a typical interpretation suggesting that she knew I wanted her help and knew what she could do: "You wanted me to throw you a line." And the session was over.

After the session, I reminded myself that analytical sessions were different from the psychotherapy sessions I had been used to, this to calm myself and prepare for the coming year. And from this first session, I deduced that the rules were not going to change during the termination period. There still would be no social time. No talk of the weather, which in Iowa seemed a habitual necessity. There would still be long periods of silence, and her words would continue to be puzzling. The relationship with her was unlike any other relationship I have ever experienced. I remember the feeling, the knowing, the absolute certainty that she agreed with my decision of using a year for termination even though she did not say it directly. Her response elicited the type of sensation, the sense of inner knowing, I had experienced when I discerned that I needed a year for termination. I was excited. I had eleven months and one month shy of one day remaining.

Later in the week, during my contemplation time at home, it became clear to me that when I'd experienced this type of inner knowing in the past, I would have categorized it as inexplicable and then promptly ignored it. I would have thought it not worth examining. This was a way I had continued to disregard my inner life for many years. Wrestling my entire life with a yearning for both contemplative meditative time and having deep connections, intimacy with others, I mostly landed on the side of the social so as not to let others down, so it was not a frequent occurrence to recognize an inner message. I wanted to learn from the termination process how to pay attention to my inner knowing.

I knew that while the contemplative spiritual part of me was not buried deep in the mud during my time in psychoanalysis, it was covered by a layer of sand such as could be shaken off a beach towel, sand that could be discarded when one needed to go deeper and touch into the sacred. Entering Freudian psychoanalysis at the age of sixty-two had initiated a time period when I chose to let the towel remain largely stationary. It was as if I knew unconsciously that I could always remove the sand from the towel. I didn't know consciously yet that during the termination year, I would find myself vigorously shaking the towel.

During the coming week, I thought about letting go of analysis. I was able to acknowledge that the metaphorical fruits I had gathered were many, but found myself facing another dichotomy. Facing me was the struggle of choosing between my contemplative nature (that appeared to be developing as I enjoyed a consistent meditation practice) or my social yearnings that historically had kept me saying yes to invitations for group gatherings when I really wanted to say no. In addition, there was another dilemma, one that would challenge my all-or-nothing thinking: I continued vacillating between feelings of revulsion and feelings of admiration for

Sigmund Freud, the person. In an effort to come to terms with my dilemma, I kept buying books about Freud. However, I was confused by the variety of opinions I encountered. There were varying reflections of him as a person and clinician depending on whether or not the critic took into account the stage of Freud's writing. It was difficult to sort out and integrate Freud's continually developing theories. He did not go back to revise his work; he kept writing. My shelf was full.

The knowledge that I was terminating, for some reason, most likely my unconscious making itself known again, made it feel imperative I continue to research for myself who Freud was. The family therapist part of me wanted to know his sibling position and family background. The feminist in me wanted to know how he felt about women. The budding psychoanalytic part of me wanted to understand the man who created the system that had trained my analyst so she could be of such enormous benefit to me. When I was learning to meditate in the Zen tradition, I learned about koans—Zen riddles that will bring on Enlightenment if you solve them. At times, the psychoanalyst's specially formulated interpretations appeared designed as my private koans to solve. Like puzzling on a koan, her words challenged me to understand them in order to become more conscious. There was a feeling of uncertainty when struggling with the Zen koans I encountered in Buddhist literature. It was the type of uncertainty I often felt when hearing my analyst's interpretations.

Freud described uncertainty as "the blindness of the seeing eye" (Petrucelli, 2010). I cautiously felt that I understood this but wondered when I was without regular sessions of Freudian psychoanalysis helping explore my inner life, how would I continue to experience the blindness of the seeing eye? (Petrucelli, 2010). And most of all, I wanted to know what the creator of psychoanalysis thought about religion and spirituality. My first realization that it was time to let go of my four times a week sessions and be on my own had brought on more questions than I had expected. Thankfully, I had a calendar year. I hoped it was enough.

2

OPPOSITION

December 2019

I shiver despite being covered with a red synthetic blanket, a blanket Denae conscientiously provides, a blanket that my inchoate consciousness bemoans has more qualities of the secular than the sacred. A blanket for all her patients. Remembering Freud's belief that humans have a strong tendency towards the pleasure-principle validates the need for my own blanket, a blanket made of natural fibers, a divine blanket that was only for my use when lying on the analytical couch. I tried not to ruminate about my wish, a wish that spoke of my immature desire. I remembered her curt response when I naively spoke of this a few years ago. Referring to my wish as a 'big want,' she made certain I realized that wants were related to childhood needs, needs extended into adulthood: most notably, my need to be special and my need to be comfortable. Before analysis, these needs had been too commonplace to view as problematic.

Taking matters into my own hands (desiring to be comfortable for the 50-minute session), I pull my down-filled puffer coat over me as an additional coverlet. While making this adjustment, I uncover a blest bit of ambivalence: this was the final December of psychoanalytic treatment, and I was happy and sad! Growing more used to the feeling of feeling feelings after years of analyst goading, I began to enter my annual angst-fest, which was the result of her yearly holiday departure during Christmas and New Year. This year I noted with pride the dread I was experiencing was slightly diminished. My awareness that she was not going to be available for our scheduled routine had previously felt comparable to an infant being left starving by the side of the road. I recall the habitual disagreement we encountered: her steadfast refusal to reveal out of the office plans versus my adamant plea for knowledge of her out of the office whereabouts.

The details from the early years of my well-thought out tactics to entice her to tell me are hazy and now appear to my more fully developed analyzed self as controlling and slightly immature, not to mention omnipotent.

"You thought you could force me to tell you where I was going."

Her voice tone is an octave higher than usual when she refreshes my memory by sharing this observation. I sense it was an effort to maintain her neutral analytic composure when slipping in the detail regarding the certainty I had possessed, thinking I could force her to tell me where she was going. She sounds tickled with being able to tell me that she knew of my certainty and sure that I will find it amusing. Our subsequent laughter intensifies when I mention that I have long since given up caring about her whereabouts. This sharing of my dismissal of feelings about her whereabouts she would diagnose as reaction formation—the idea that one adopts the opposite stance from what one actually feels as a defense against feelings one does not want to feel. But she let it go this time, I speculate, in the spirit of the season.

Despite the illusion that my lessened angst about her absence at the end of December was holding fast, during the last session of the month, trying to make my words sound not ridiculous but amusing, I felt driven to comment that it would not be a complete December without me asking her where she was going on her two weeks out of the office. "You didn't ask me for a lot of years," she said, which made me mad as I did not like her saying "a lot of years" because it made it sound like I had been in treatment forever, which of course was accurate, but I did not appreciate her saying it. But to my credit, at least I recognized the discomfort I felt hearing the reality of my numerous sessions, reality being what Freud insisted on uncovering and sticking to. I valiantly try to accept reality, not oppose it. During this last December I will ever be in psychoanalysis.

But another reason I was mad when she said this was because what I heard was, "Even though you didn't ask, I knew you wanted to ask," implying that wanting to ask was as problematic as asking. It felt like I couldn't win.

Feeling the shame of childishly wanting to know her whereabouts when she was out of the office, I took precious session time to process these feelings. I was silent for several breaths. I was startled when what had begun to feel like sacred space was rudely interrupted by her question. "What do you imagine?"

The former psychotherapist in me did not appreciate her asking this because her words felt as if they were taken out of a second-rate melodramatic script; I deemed them so obvious as to have been laughable. The words sound Jungian is the first thought that crossed my mind. I expect more from her. I decide to humor her, and assume she was asking for what I imagined her doing on her time off, so I answered, "I picture you flying off to Paris or staying home reading your Freud's Standard Set." Knowing she owned such a treasure felt transgressive, but if questioned, I would have been quick to point out she had uncharacteristically revealed this tidbit to me one day when we were discussing my interest in psychoanalytic literature, with her, of course, making certain to reinforce her opinion that my job as her patient was not to read about psychoanalysis but to experience psychoanalysis.

Wanting the session to gravitate to a deeper level of insight, not imagination, not willing to give up any of my precious books (I did not yet own the entire series of Freud's work), I stayed in the silence that followed voicing my imaginings, which predictably she left floating in the cold psychoanalytic air. Lying on the couch and reflecting inwardly, doing what was expected in the psychoanalytic process, I discern that my answers appear, at least in my humble opinion, more sophisticated than my usual responses. I grin to myself and leap, unconsciously of course, right into my old pattern of feeling above it all, more in touch with wisdom than the average person. These gems, I muse, must have evolved from a new part of me that is part of my transformation. As this becomes more evident to me, I skillfully dodge my usual defensive filters and surprise myself by saying out loud: "I thought being different would be different."

"You thought that being different would mean you would be split off from yourself." After working with me for so many years, I think she knew how entranced I was about being perfect and getting everything right. And I think she also knew how my spiritual side was an integral part of me and that I would not be Nicky without that part. She probably knew that I was worried about losing or splitting off from my spiritual nature, as well as disappointed that I was not perfect.

The session drew to a close shortly after her interpretation, an interpretation that used the psychoanalytic word "split" for the first time I could remember and implied something I could not quite grab hold of yet. I left the room offering no response but would continue to reflect on her words for quite some time. Occasionally when sessions were over, I plum forgot what she had said and other times did not understand what she had meant, but this time, I heard, remembered, and wanted to think about what she had offered. What was she meaning about being split off from myself?

Later that evening, lying snuggled in my own warm bed with this question in mind, I opened to the associative way, known as free association, a technique I had learned to sometimes practice during my time actually with the analyst. In the early days of my psychoanalytic treatment, I had exhibited strong opposition to this way of gaining knowledge by planning my associations. (Freud would connect it with resistance).

Now, snuggled in my own bed, indoctrinated by over a decade of couch time, I allowed my mind to float dreamily without succumbing to sleep. It was not long before this message surfaced: the analyst was implying I had mistakenly anticipated transformation meant that my old patterns would be gone—split off. I bet she assumed (quite correctly) that I also believed I would not have to deal with dysfunctional habits any longer. Curling up in the fetal position, considering my transformation nearly complete, trusting I was basically a new person, I sleepily realized that these thoughts were a remnant of my tendency to think in terms of black and white. When I said I was surprised change felt different from my expectations. What I didn't know consciously was that I was disappointed the dysfunctional part of me was still hanging around. Now I stretched to my full length under the covers in an effort to relax and begin going to sleep. I noted that now I had empathy for myself while at the same time appreciating the reality that I was not the perfect person I wanted to be.

Relaxation was settling in as I assured myself this was what she meant by splitting from myself. It fit with all I had learned in psychoanalysis and made sense to me. I repeated to myself that my former mistaken notion of hope would have been, if I changed, an end to all my problems. I forgave myself for this way of thinking even though when I blurted out that I thought change would feel different, I did not have a clear awareness of what that meant. My speculation was that these words had their origin in my unconscious, and I began to marvel at how many layers our minds have. Freud was ahead of his time, I mused.

Slipping into the dream state, an image appears in my mind of a black-and-white, deckle-edged photo of me at twelve years old while I was attending Clear Lake United Methodist Church Camp. I am standing beside a young man who appears very relaxed and happy, exactly my height, features suggesting he was Asian Indian. I insist on bringing this exotic visitor home to introduce him to my local church congregation.

I remain with the image and remember how I did not recognize my fascination with him as a romantic attraction. The powerful feelings that led me to drag him home to speak to my church community and to meet my parents, to experience our 80 acres of farmland, I suspected had to do with the internal flutters I had felt hearing him speak with a charming accent, observing his physical body expressing grace and ease, learning later this was a contemplative stance. His pungent smell, a smell that I imagined was due to spices not found in my mother's kitchen. I remembered how my deep desire had been to understand the abundance of joy and life he exuded. There is no recollection of what he said, but using my imagination, I picture him smiling at me and asking questions in an effort to understand my culture as I ask him questions about his family and his village.

This connection, this brief relationship, undoubtedly was

the beginning of a lifelong infatuation with India, resulting in visits to India four times. Researching the differences between Western ways of being in the world, a style people might say is dominated by the conscious mind, opposed to Eastern culture that some describe as being in touch with the unconscious, meant reading everything my adult self could find on the profound differences in thought and behavior between living from the conscious mind rather than the unconscious mind.

Still snuggling in my warm bed drifting off to sleep, savoring my introduction to India, I return to the question of what the analyst was implying by using the word split.

Ruminating on her word, split, reminds me of an internal split I have noticed during this termination year. I want to integrate the reality-based ideas I picked up in treatment with what I consider my spiritual nature. Captivated by the thought of commingling my spiritual proclivities with what I have gleaned from psychoanalysis excites me. I hope to do this in a more integrated manner.

But did she mean there was a part of me I was afraid to lose if I stayed true to Freud's reality as I wove it into my life? Disregarding for a moment the analyst's words, I begin checking my own thoughts, tapping into the fear that a split might mean I would I have to give up my traditional oldest daughter persona, a role that I was reforming and restructuring in analysis, a part that had served me well. Or would the transformation lead me to abandon the part of me that thrilled to sit along bare walls with Zen meditators in my sangha? Or would I devise a way that all of these parts could coalesce, and all be me?

As December continued to unfold and analytical time slipped away, we received a phone call that my husband's older brother Mike, had died. Sad though not devastated as I had not known him long, I flashed on an interaction that occurred when Wendell and I visited him and his wife in Florida shortly after our marriage in 2009. After welcoming us to their home, they profusely apologized for plumbing problems, which, while they did not directly affect us, seemingly made entertaining more difficult for them. As Mike was loading up our suitcases on our last day, I complimented him for not letting the plumbing problems interfere and for being such a good host. "It's just what we do," was his response.

I was surprised by his words and surreptitiously stepped farther down the driveway toward the street instead of following through on my previous impulse to move forward and hug him. His remark, which I heard as a retort, set me back on my heels because it did not address my need to be special. I felt rebuffed by his words. But because of what I was learning in psychoanalysis, I was able to sense the reason for my reaction. I had felt his words kept me at arm's length. This awareness was not in time to overcome my unconscious reaction of backing away, so there was no embrace as I had imagined. Now that would never happen.

The drive to attend his memorial was uneventful. During the service held at a mortuary, it was evident that many people had benefited from what he "just did for them." He was a well-loved man. There were tributes, laughter, flowers, and tears. Throughout the day, feeling a bit the outsider knowing only a handful of people there, I began to face my own mortality, the inevitable human challenge. I would die too. Even though I warmed to the Christian prayers and hymns, they felt like comfort from the past. During the dark and stormy drive home, I began to realize that the death of my husband's brother was continuing to dismantle the existential denial I had identified during analysis that placed me in the position of being above it all.

I wanted to believe that this confrontation with my mortality would lead to feelings of compassion and to finally reading the *Tibetan Book of the Dead* that I had purchased years ago. Maybe the analyst, when she spoke of splitting, had been predicting my pattern of thinking that I could easily split off from my oppositional ways as well as deny my fear of death. My tendency to confront and oppose anything that I did not totally understand or control, while not as strong, was not gone. Perhaps it would never go away entirely.

Home safely from our trip, I resumed my last December of psychoanalytical treatment with a sense of gratitude. Analysis was winding down; I was feeling less oppositional. However, the knowledge that in ten months I would not be in analysis any longer continued to heighten my curiosity about Sigmund Freud, the creator of psychoanalysis. I wanted to know more about him and the psychoanalytic method I credited for my new interior freedom. What if ideas came up in my reading that I needed help to understand? I thought to myself how difficult it was to ask my analyst questions.

Once again, I recalled how she wanted me to experience psychoanalysis with her acting as the analyst and not rely on psychoanalytic books. I stubbornly believed that if I read Freud's work and studied what psychoanalytic techniques other experts suggested, while I was wise enough to know it wouldn't cure me, I believed the knowledge would speed up the process. I was so certain I was right.

This oppositional decision that reading would enhance my experience in psychoanalysis brought me to a startling conclusion: Freud and I had things in common. I did not really appreciate this thought—you could say I opposed this notion—but since it came to me unasked and I have learned to pay attention to messages of this type, I decided to use it as a focus for my research.

I discovered that Freud and I at the beginning of our careers shared the conventional belief that knowledge was primarily intellectual. I believed, like he did, that if facts were known, especially about causation, change would transpire. Freud initially thought if he could explain to his patients what had happened in their development and speculate with them about how this was lodged in their unconscious, they would be cured. Freud rapidly learned the flaw in his thinking: intellectual knowledge as such does not produce change.

That is what my analyst knew that I did not fully understand for many years. It would not be enough for me to read about psychoanalysis; I had to experience it. Feel the uncomfortable feelings. Thinking about it was not enough. Like in my meditation practice, I had to feel my breath, not just observe it. In analysis, I had to learn that discovering one's unconscious does not happen intellectually. For me, there usually was a great deal of anxiety that occurred before an affective experience could lead to change. I resisted. However, when I could allow myself to feel my feelings, calm the anxiety, make the unconscious, conscious, it changed how I thought about the world. It is difficult to put these types of experiences into words.

I wondered how many more difficult feelings would I have to face? What would I find out when continuing to study Freud and his method of psychoanalysis? Would changing continue to feel different from what I had imagined?

3

DEATH

January 2020

Knowing this was my last January in psychoanalytic treatment was a relief: no more risking life and hip fracture traversing the analyst's icy parking lot four times a week. During our first session of the year, on January 6, 2020, the analyst proposes a strategic intervention remarkably different from her usual offering of silence or non-directive questions, suggesting I carry a little snack-baggy of kitty litter in my purse, a commonsense directive that astonishes me enough that my ego skids around its usual oppositional nature, deciding to try it. The only alteration in her instructions is to substitute ice-melt, for I, alas, have no kittens in my home. Despite grave misgivings, I find my sense of confidence bolstered as I grab the sack from my coat pocket on January 17, 2020, the first icy day, and sprinkle salt in front of my boots. After this first successful sprinkle, I waved the snack-sized bag of ice-melt in front of her face as I strolled triumphantly to the analytical couch.

While I rejoiced that I had a new trick up my sleeve to counter the dangers of winter, death made itself known. Within a three-week period, two of my daughters-in-law lost one of their parents, neither of whom I had met. I observe, with what I presume qualifies as a psychoanalytic attitude, that I memorialized these losses by saying they 'lost' a parent. This, a phrase that in the past had seemed humorous, now raised a level of concern because while I did not want to write they lost them—lost as in couldn't find their car keys—I did not feel comfortable saying they died. I wondered if researching Freud's insights into death would help me understand my reluctance. I note to myself that I am increasingly looking to Freud. Perhaps termination is more of an event than I am admitting.

As if my bonus daughter Anna (my husband's daughter from his first marriage) knew my growing obsession with Freud, she has mailed to me a stunning portrait of Freud. The artist has depicted Freud's expression as one that could be read in any number of ways, and I have hung it on the wall above my oversized monitor. I note that his expression appears alternately stern, puzzled, concerned, or sad, depending, of course, on my mood. I marvel at how mind-boggling it is that my perception of the image couldn't be a clearer demonstration of Freud's concept of projection—the idea that we project what is inside of us onto the external world.

Being aware that only nine months of analysis glimmer ahead of me adds fuel to my already burning desire to learn more about psychoanalysis. I want to give birth to myself as a new creation. The turbulent ideas in my unconscious are at last becoming more conscious, because not only did I discern but also admit to myself an uncomfortable truth: I want the analyst to be impressed by all I know about Freud and psychoanalysis.

This self-confession, uncomfortable as it is, doesn't

interfere with my reading and buying books, mostly used books, but I occasionally splurge for a new pristine copy. I joke to my husband that I cannot die until I read them all, surprising myself with another reference to endings and death. Was I unconsciously hoping that if I bought enough books I would not die? It was impossible to fully explain the intensity I felt about understanding the theory my analyst used. Now I specifically wanted to learn about how psychoanalytic theory regarded death.

My first discovery did not relate directly to the subject of death, but the literature indicates it was one of Freud's greatest creations: the analytic attitude. I recognize immediately this was the attitude my analyst, both to my consternation and admiration, adheres to without ceasing throughout my years in her care as an analysand. Since Freud did not leave a succinct definition of the analytic attitude, I join countless others who have, over the decades, tried to discern what he was proposing. I wanted to do this in order to articulate and provide a clear answer for doubters and all those interested in his theory. This was an arduous answer to pin down because Freud's actions with his own patients varied widely from his written instructions about the guidelines for how to treat analysands.

My analyst seemed clear about what the analytic attitude was for her. Here's what I observed. She was always present, but not personal. No small talk. She listened closely to everything that I said and arranged the facts in story form, then repeated it to me, accenting some parts and ignoring others. She was continually on the lookout for emotions, especially the ones that were present in the session that I did not want to acknowledge. She stayed neutral while at the same time indicated she understood the complexity and ambiguity connected with any change I was thinking of making. She maintained a respectful, affirmative attitude at all times. I tried to do all these things with my clients and can report that they are harder to consistently carry out than you might think.

As I said earlier, I realized that Freud and I jointly believed that healing would happen if patients were presented with the facts, but I had been blissfully unaware of how personally similar Freud and I were in the way we managed differences and in how stubborn we both were—sometimes for the good and other times for ill. It pains me to say I did not like him because he was mirroring traits in myself that I had not yet rescued from my unconscious, but looking back, that is the truth as I see it now. I was drawn to Freud's analytic attitude as a way of thinking because it made life fascinating and rich; at the same time, it was an attitude I periodically felt in opposition to because it made life so complicated. There were so many layers to explore. The analytic attitude often brought to mind an idea I previously had mostly avoided: we were all going to die. I was stunned to read that Freud announced that he was close to death, or resigned to death, when he was in his thirties.

I was acutely aware that I was going to be seventy-five on my next October birthday. This milestone would mean I would be the age my mother was when she died on my birthday twenty-plus years ago. As if to complete a circle, she breathed her last breath at nearly the same clock time she had given birth to me. This awareness of being alive at the same age she was when she died made me face mortality in a new way. But perhaps unconsciously, I believed that as long as I could keep my interest in psychoanalysis alive, buy enough books, I would not age. As long as my body kept functioning well.

Continuing my research on Freud, I opened to the index of a book in my library to search for Sigmund's name, and as part of the process, spied a note dated January 4, 2011, which was written on the back blank page of the book. This was two years after my father's death. I must have had this book in hand when I heard this tidbit from my brother and wanted to remember. Words that brought back to mind what Nolan, my only brother, told me our dad had said to him before he died: "How much more do I have to endure till we get out of this life?" I called my brother to see if he remembered more about what Dad had said. Nolan remembered feeling that Dad was implying bad things happening in the world was what he no longer wanted to endure but did not remember the context of when Dad said this. Personally, I wondered if Dad suffered more than I had realized.

As the month progressed, ideas about death continued softly surrounding me. I had read that ending analysis might arouse anxieties about death (Kantrowitz, 2015). I wondered if that was what was happening to me?

I knew Freud wrote about the death instinct or the death drive, but that was not where my interest was focused when I began. The social worker in me wanted to investigate how Freud personally had managed dealing with the dying process since throughout many years of his life, he was convinced that he was dying (Roiphe, 2016). The literature described how Freud spent several decades thinking about how to die. To him, the ideal death happened because you maintained 'heroic clarity,' which meant that you were rational, that you allowed yourself to apprehend, fully and with all your senses, the process of death. The alternative to 'heroic clarity' was unthinkable for Freud: to fear death, to deny it, to rage against it, to be, in other words, out of control (Roiphe, 2016). Of course, Freud saw 'heroic clarity' as a goal for all of life, not just at the very end, which is when it is more difficult to maintain.

Freud was diagnosed with throat cancer in April 1923 and at that time wrote modestly that there was nothing he could say about this illness that would not be expected. He continued somewhat less diffident in his manner: "The uncertainty that hovers over a man of sixty-seven has now found its material expression." This statement indicates to me not only was he interested in the structure of the mind, but he was also curious how the mind and body were interconnected. Freud's investigations of how the mind and body were connected, now known as psychosomatics, was short lived; however, his struggle with cancer was long, lasting sixteen years. He died at the age of eighty-three.

I remembered my own brush with illness. When I could not walk in 2016 at the age of seventy-one, I decided I was ready to die. I did not want to go through the suffering that I thought was in store for me. I did not think I would ever recuperate, so I thought I might as well call my adult children home, say goodbye, and die. I thought about not having to worry about anything anymore. There was some appeal to this choice. I think Freud would have said that I was under the power, had succumbed to the death instinct.

I suddenly remembered how my psychoanalyst had stepped out of her strict analytical attitude of neutrality and became instrumental in me opting for what the surgeon informed me was a procedure. I had said, let's call it what it is— an operation or, if you don't like that, surgery. I recalled how in response to my garbled presentation to her of the options in front of me, she had asked: "Why wouldn't you try the surgery?" Her question felt biased in favor of medical intervention. I was so angry when I heard her utter those words that I did not recognize them initially as caring.

All the surgeries Freud had undergone for his throat cancer came to mind. After the operations, he had refused medication for his pain, saying that he wanted to be clearheaded to the end of his life. This was the heroic clarity he strove to embody in life.

In 2016, I denied being afraid of death. I knew I was afraid of physical suffering. The ideal of 'heroic clarity' had tantalized me. I had wanted to be a hero. I wanted to be rational and brave and make Freud proud. So, while I was not consciously raging against death and did not consciously fear death, in wanting to die, I was using death as an escape. This was a cowardly way out of my dilemma. Luckily, I had learned in the decade of psychoanalysis to pay attention to reality. When I had looked at the facts, the reality was that I had a chance for healing and returning to normalcy, though the odds for success were not good as they had been for cataract surgery. I had wanted to be courageous like Freud was. I was lucky that what the surgeon had called a procedure worked for me. After a period of recovery, I returned to normal life.

But now it was 2020, and I was once again contemplating ideas about death. But this time I wasn't using thoughts of death as an escape. Instead, I kept remembering that it was January, a new year; just saying 2020 out loud made me think about my eyes and the upcoming cataract surgery for my left eye at the end of the month. My left eye had suffered from optic neuropathy, probably caused by a virus years ago. This condition meant that for years I could not see color in the world if I covered over my right eye, which I sometimes did to give myself a faux psychedelic experience of the world looking different, as I'd heard people experience when they ingested LSD. Though I have never been under the influence of drugs purported to give otherworldly experiences, I was fascinated with what I had read or heard from others. Seeing the unseen had a spiritual aspect I longed for. The fear of injuring my body and of long-term damage protected me from further exploration.

The ophthalmologist who specialized in cataract surgery informed me we would start on January 29, 2020, with the problematic eye, my left eye, clarifying that he would not be able to repair the optic nerve damage. After describing multiple hazards and problems that could occur, he speculated my vision in that eye would improve. I was glad that psychoanalysis had helped me tune into reality so I could hear the hazards without freaking out and know that he had to utter those warnings and that most likely they would not happen. Surgery would begin with the compromised eye so that just in case something untoward should occur, I would still have my good eye.

It seemed ironic to me that the year 2020, 20/20 being the usual way of talking about perfect eyesight, was the year for the removal of my cataracts, the death of an opaque layer that was blurring my view of the world. I knew it would be an ordeal to deal with drops after each surgery, but I knew Wendell would help me. I was so grateful that I didn't have to go through these surgeries alone and since I was getting more comfortable with dealing with reality, as Freud preached, I studied the statistics about cataract surgeries and felt there was a good chance that all would go well.

Since I was tuned into the idea that twenty-first century cataract surgery was as common as having your tonsils out, I spent very little time worrying about the surgeries. In frigid January sessions when my analyst's parking lot was covered with ice, I felt it was generous of me to humor the various vision metaphors she seemed unable to resist. These metaphors sometimes irritated me, like when she responded I did not want to see clearly when I retorted that I did not understand what she said. This felt unfair as my perception had her muttering under her breath, impossible to hear. Using another metaphor that mixed the physical with the psychological, she suggested that if things were not clear-cut, my pattern was to retreat. Initially, I heartily opposed both interpretations. She had some nerve, I thought, using my medical condition that way. However, as the cold dark January days unfolded, I began to remember all that I had learned from my analysis. I also began noticing the unvarnished truth of her words and wondered, what else was going to be revealed?

4

Awakening

February 2020

The fourth month of the year-long termination process has begun. Each day this month when I wake up, I open my eyes and give thanks for modern day cataract surgery. I am so grateful; I can now see the clock across the room without putting on my glasses. Some mornings I tap into psychoanalytic wisdom—the past is in the present—and recall the first time I wore prescription lenses in elementary school and could see that a tree was not a solid blob of green but was made up of individual leaves. The current change in my vision feels almost as dramatic. Colors look brighter and clearer. Everything feels easier now without cataract cloudiness.

I have learned from Freudian analysis how to be rational, but as I open to a broader view that includes what we cannot see, I am intuiting that rational thought can coexist with other forms of awareness. In this new expanded way of viewing the world, I contemplate how ordinary actions can serve as metaphors and thus add more meaning to life. This type of spirituality is not religious, as in going to church. It is more that I can discern how everything could be seen by some as completely secular and just what it is, nothing more. This, the materialistic view of life. And yet at the same time, everything could be seen as sacred—having layers of meaning and hints of the transcendent while still maintaining the idea that matter, matters. My new way of observing life adds meaning, it doesn't take anything away.

My nighttime dreams are becoming clearer and more intense since cataract surgery though I don't know if there is a connection—enhancement of dream content was not listed as a benefit or side effect. Reading Adam Phillips, a prolific psychoanalytic author who challenges me to see things in a psychoanalytic way, I learn Freud thought dreams were the way we give voice to our secret desires. My dreams are undoubtedly full of metaphors and symbols that I haven't taken time to decode. The dream, according to Freud, represents the impenetrable privateness of the Self. My need for privacy when it came to my analytical work had a sacred feel to it.

That is until I decided to write a memoir about my more than a decade of psychoanalysis. Before that, I didn't mention, even to close friends or family, that I was in analysis or that I was doing dreamwork. When I did tell others about what felt like very personal and embarrassing topics I was working on in analysis, it was surprising and comforting that many times they understood. Often, they would generously relate similar examples from their own lives. It is the missionary self that wanted me to travel to Africa as a teenager and tell people what to believe. Writing a memoir came out of my need to help others see that transformation is possible, but to do so, I needed to be willing to share what is usually not shared.

My research continues as the month slips away. Many days, I wake before dawn and spend time cradling the fuzzy intuition that appeared during the night. Full of intensity, it demands early morning attention. Its message implies that the initial referral request for depth psychotherapy, the one made many years ago, heralded from my innate inner spiritual seeker. I have not linked the beginning of analysis with my spiritual sense, a set of feelings that have been reverberating in my psyche for months begging for more space.

As the sun rises through the trees and I snuggle in bed, I dive into the suggestion that the spiritual seeker was behind my yearning for analysis and recall how after an initial session with the analyst, nothing could stop me from working with her. As a psychotherapist myself, the manner in which she interacted with me piqued my curiosity about technique. I was intrigued. It was as if when I was with her, I was awake with a new intensity. She was comfortable with silence and there was an enticing ceremonial way she conducted herself as she greeted me from behind a screen and ushered me into her consultation room. I grin as I ponder this new realization that what I was looking for when I signed up for Freudian psychoanalysis was connected to my lifelong search for spirituality. I don't fully understand it yet but feelings of excitement tell me that there is something about this intuition that is true.

I tumble out of bed and reflect that each month I appreciate more and more the meditative dimension in psychoanalysis. On the rare occasions the analyst and I observe silence for a longer than normal time or laugh spontaneously together, it feels to me a type of prayer. Since the termination year has begun, surprisingly I feel more tuned into the spiritual world, paying attention to sacred feelings that have always been second nature to me. The sacred having diverse meanings, but ultimately, anything qualifies that remains still long enough for me to touch its essence. I confess that for more than a decade these occurrences have barely found acknowledgment or expression because unconsciously (I was unaware of this action) I placed spiritual yearning on the back burner. This was essentially because of my loyalty to Freud, believing he was against any type of spiritual or religious feeling.

When I discover in my research that Freud supports the idea that religious feelings are important in people's lives, I feel myself awakening to all varieties of experience that have previously not garnered acknowledgment. The more I open, the more I notice synchronicities that Carl Jung wrote about. I have gifted myself with books that speak to my questions. The latest draw is to the book *Being Spiritual But Not Religious*. I am captivated by the title; the book accurately describes me. Looking at the cover, I feel a sense of strange relief that I no longer go to church. If being religious means I need to believe in shared, public, or institutional expressions or express a belief in the existence of a being that is beyond the physical world, I want no part of it.

Another enticement to this book is the editor, William B. Parsons, a professor of religion at Rice University. Dr. Parsons and I have never met in person, though it almost seems inevitable we will at some point because of the strong connection I sense between us. When I have reached out to him through email, expressing appreciation for his books, he has responded. Through this correspondence, I learn that Parsons joins me in being enamored by the person Sigmund Freud and by Freud's creation, psychoanalysis. We are both curious about Freud's connection to religion, especially the phrase Freud reportedly uttered to explain one of his hard to define experiences: oceanic feeling. This is a phrase that Parsons wrote a book about and a phrase that would periodically go in and out of my memory causing no end of amusement and speculation on my part for the reasons this continued to occur. I would be ready to comment on this to the analyst and find the word unavailable in my mind. Both Parsons and I show interest in, as indeed Freud did, greater self-awareness.

Having this connection with Parsons, another writer, especially a writer with an interest in Freud and religion, is a rare privilege. I realize in today's world, many people believe Freud was dismissive of religion but after studying Parsons's research, I discover how Parsons remains open to observing changes that took place in Freud's theoretical development over the years, changes many writers ignore. I appreciate how Parsons's research continues to uncover data suggesting Freud was not totally against religion. Parsons takes into account how translators attempt to make psychoanalysis scientific by using the word *mind* to replace Freud's German word for soul. In *Freud and Man's Soul*, Bruno Bettelheim comments that reading Freud's work in German gives one the feeling of the essential humanism of Freud's work. Bettelheim writes that through Freud's own struggles, he showed us how the soul could become aware of itself (Bettelheim, 1982).

Sometimes I feel as if I am living a double life. Excitement about what I am learning about Freud and the discipline of psychoanalysis keeps me glued to the page while at the same time I deal with a compulsion to hide all evidence from my analyst and not let free associations touch on what I read. And then there is my double life when it comes to the sacred and the secular. My mostly unconscious decision to place what is conventionally seen as sacred aside is fighting with the urge to welcome it all and feel more connected to others and to Nature. The analyst's recommendation that I should experience psychoanalysis, not read about it, is never far from my mind. Despite all this, I stubbornly keep reading. I cannot resist learning all I can about the founder of the process that helps me change dysfunctional patterns.

In my research, I do free association off the couch. One book leads to another and then another. After reading an article by Christine Downing, a scholar, educator, and author in the fields of mythology, religion, depth psychology and feminist studies, I searched for everything I could get my hands on that she had published. I felt resonance with her views on Freud, and I trusted her scholarship. A comment from a transcribed lecture that Downing presented at San Diego State University was especially insightful. No one before Downing had assigned words to my feelings about the difference between Jung and Freud. Downing was acquainted with Carl Jung's work before she studied Freud. She wrote that Jung was a little bit too much like a soft pillow for her. Her words helped me clarify that what I had needed from my analyst was the unyielding insistence on reality. I was convinced that a Jungian analyst would not be demanding enough for my stubborn nature. Yes, I thought, I have always felt Jung wasn't clear enough about reality and focused too much on active imagination. Downing discloses she needed the particular creative spark that occurred as a result of contending with and rebelling against Freud.

Downing reports she heard Freud saying that the unconscious is not entirely made of inner experiences but is a different way of perceiving, ordering, remembering (Downing, Re-Visioning Autobiography: The Bequest of Freud and Jung). I like thinking about the unconscious as a different way of perceiving, ordering, and remembering. Freud labeled the part of our mind that creates religious or mystical feelings, 'the core of our being.' He believed these religious feelings relate to the feelings we experienced in our infancy. That in the womb we experience a nirvana-like state that we have memories of but no words for. Freud named these feelings primary process. When we were breastfed by our mothers, the feeling was so glorious, so enveloping that we did not want to ever be deprived of those feelings. Freud believed longing for these feelings lasts for our entire life. Because my analyst kept encouraging me to express feelings, especially when they were uncomfortable, I was opening up and experiencing more sensation. I was beginning to feel more open to introspection, reason, and freedom as central components of human life. My life was gaining a richness that I attributed to the analytical work though I couldn't prove what was causing the transformation that I observed.

As the sense of openness continued to evolve, I became more convinced that spirituality would find a way to incorporate itself when I left analysis. At about this same time, I read how Freud eventually became aware that any effort to do away with religion would be senseless, hopeless, and cruel. He understood that religious beliefs offer people relief from mental anguish and that devotional rituals are a safe way for people to express neurotic compulsions.

Freud had a passion for creating psychoanalysis as a scientific discipline and at the age of sixty-nine, said: "Something will come of my life's labors in the future, though I cannot myself tell whether it will be much or little" (Rubin, 1998). Freud studied classical literature and worked on unearthing the origins of religion, which he believed were located in the unconscious psychic operations of human minds. He wanted to discover what made humans do what they do. Freud preached that religious knowledge was designed to keep people in a dependent position, and that religion represented the direct opposite of evidence-based critical thought that he wanted the backbone of psychoanalysis to be.

People, he claimed, gave up their ability to take care of themselves by praying to an unseen Being, asking it to do for them what he believed they needed to do for themselves. Religion took freedom away from people, he said, so that they could not be their authentic selves. I remember as a young adult searching for the right thing to believe in and finding comfort when others agreed with what I chose and scoffing at those who chose differently. Freud wrote that religion insisted people unquestioningly accept religious dogma and that this would make psychoanalysis impossible. This was my experience in the organized church and after being challenged to think for myself in psychoanalysis, accepting dogma no longer appeals to me.

Sometimes it feels as if there is something working in me that I want to be responsible for, awake to greet and learn from, too. Perhaps it is my new appreciation of how life evolves, a new awareness of awe and the potent power of love. How can I be present to it all? The sense of spirituality that keeps unfolding as the termination year progresses has a place for multiple ways of experiencing the spiritual view of life—many ways of thinking about God, and even the definition of God is not completely settled in my mind.

My ideas about Freud and religion have been influenced by Marsha Hewitt, a professor and psychoanalyst, who writes that Freud changed the way people thought about religion. Hewitt writes that Freud is widely and unquestioningly accepted as a cantankerous atheist who denigrated religion and belittled believers. It was undoubtedly these opinions about Freud that I was exposed to, and they would go a long way to explaining why, prior to my research and experience in analysis, I was disappointed in Freud. Why I was routing for Romaine Rolland's view of the oceanic feeling as evidence of a spiritual core in humanity. However, the more research I uncover about the facts regarding Freud the person and psychoanalysis, his theory, the more open I am to his thinking. The disappointment fades as I experience and learn more.

On February 21, 2020, the following interchange occurs, which at its core relates to the place of disappointment in my psyche. This discussion took place in my analyst's office during a session that occurred before the pandemic made in-office work an experience to remember. I begin the session by saying, "I'm fighting the battle against feeling special," and as usual am gobsmacked by how her reply leaps to another level of who I am.

"Your fury is not about not being special. It's about being denied the sense of being special," to which I hastily reply, "I don't think so." Then I maturely reconsider and mutter, "It's hard for me to go there."

"I know," she says softly.

Then my sense of needing to use the bathroom becomes overwhelming so I sit up from the couch and leave. Make it to the bathroom just barely in time. When I'm peeing I have an insight: I didn't deny myself the feeling of needing to pee even though I was disappointed that I would have to miss precious minutes of my analytic session. This feels revolutionary. I need to pay attention, not cover over the first feeling of disappointment. When I rush past the disappointment, it turns to rage. It has no expression. I return to the couch and my free association goes to the rush of feeling that I tell her accompanies fifty-eight likes on Facebook.

"You were looking for feeling special."

"No, I just changed my cover photo, and I didn't know it would be a post."

Then later in the session I inform the analyst that my editor has to have cataract surgery and I exclaim heartily, "The Universe must be saying your book needs more time." There is silence. There is no response until I add, "This is good!"

"That wasn't your first response."

Hotly, I think, Yes, yes it was! Then I again decide to reconsider. "No, it wasn't—I covered over the disappointment. I covered it over—that's what I always do."

"Yes."

What will be the result if I accept what Freud called ordinary unhappiness? How will I be present for my awakening laced with disappointment? Will a sense of the spiritual continue to unfold?

5

MEETING

March 2020

The vernal equinox never arrives soon enough. March, the fifth month of my yearlong termination process, signals that the end of analysis is drawing closer. Spring is closer. I need more sun and warmer weather. Now my challenge is meeting muddy patches on the nature trail near my home, places that make walking the path treacherous and contribute to a feeling of stuckness like I experienced as a girl growing up on a farm. On our 80 acres when snow melted it would dissolve into the thawing dirt creating sticky mud that grabbed onto our boots, making walking precarious. This memory illustrates how my past continues to meet me in the present, a present where continuous consumption of Freudian psychoanalytic literature is reaching a saturation point. Feeling the likelihood of being sucked into long, convoluted sentences and weary of deciphering complicated psychoanalytic words, I want to move on to something different. Thankfully, healing is continuing in my post-cataract eyes, making it easy to scan the plethora of books on my shelf and pick out ones by Buddhist authors. This will provide a different view of things, I hope.

I feel refreshed as I separate Buddhist authors from literature by Freud and about Freud. In this process, I meet books with tantalizing titles: *The Four Immeasurables: Practices to Open the Heart; True Perception: The Path of Dharma Art;* and *When Things Fall Apart: Heart Advice for Difficult Times.* Rescuing them from the shelf, I begin to feel the encouragement these titles offer, their commonsense advice on how to become unstuck and live a good life. Skimming inside these Buddhist books, I find new to me ideas on Buddhism and learn about Buddhist psychology. My previous experience while reading Buddhist authors was impatience with what seemed overly simplistic language explaining something I already knew. Now surprisingly, the words draw me in.

I begin to pay attention to my impatience and remind myself of Freud's reality principle: Don't expect to experience pleasure all the time! I find that as I slow down and absorb the words coming from this other worldview instead of rushing through them looking for an absolute answer, I am touching in on a philosophy that I can respect. When I begin to feel critical of Buddhist writing, I remember how sentences in the psychoanalytic literature are irritatingly long, loaded with obtuse psychoanalytic jargon. This new type of paying attention leads to a confrontation with my perfectionistic part. I remind myself that nothing is perfect. In Freudian psychoanalysis I learn to keep my eyes open to meeting the whole. Buddhists name this wholeness, non-dualism, or the middle way.

Even though I know slowing my pace will be a world-changing challenge, to give myself motivation, I recall that previously I had intentionally put into practice the concept of ambivalence. The word ambivalence holds a key to Freud's way of managing tensions that are part of life. Sometimes I am more successful than others at this endeavor. Meeting and incorporating the word ambivalence in my everyday life helps me remember that I don't have to cling to my former all-or-nothing thinking. My old thinking makes one thing bad or wrong and another good or right. On good days, I recognize there are features in both psychoanalytic and Buddhist literature that I appreciate and that in both, there are features I struggle with. I am no longer so intent on looking for the perfect set of principles.

Looking back on my years lying on the analytical couch, I see how the ambivalence I held concerning the word spiritual is beginning to be more conscious, therefore more subject to change. I am drawn to the word ambivalence, as well as repelled by the word. I didn't realize in November of last year, the onset of the termination year, that what seemed an expanded timeframe would truly be necessary if I was going to deal seriously with my ambivalent feelings about the sacred or as I also name it, the spiritual. I remain stubbornly loyal to rumors I heard about Freud's thoughts on religion: basically, he didn't like it. I was not yet taking into account that religion and spirituality could be two different things. I was hoping that becoming familiar with the principles of the Buddhist world would teach me another way of thinking about the spiritual.

I have been a paying member of Susan Piver's Open Heart Project for several years, meditating with her recorded meditation prompts most every morning. I like that she doesn't proselytize Buddhism but speaks about meditation as a spiritual path and says no one in the group needs to become a Buddhist. According to Piver, meditation is not just for stress reduction or increased concentration but offers a spiritual aspect. I struggle knowing what she means by spiritual and for the most part, ignore her when she uses the word. I'd always thought for a person to be spiritual they had to believe in God or be Christian and have a relationship with Jesus or the Christ.

I also appreciate how Piver combines meditation with creative writing and offers retreats for group members. In 2011, I made the decision to attend her Fearless Meditation and Writing, a workshop held at Red Feather Lakes, CO. It was the first retreat where I held no expectations of God. In my former life, mostly during my first marriage when I took part in retreat type activities offered by the United Methodist Church, before leaving my home, I would pray for God to make an appearance during the retreat so I would know I was on the right track. By then, I was ready to attend a secular retreat and look for results of concentration in meditation.

Meeting with Piver in person showed me how much courage she has to use colorful language, telling us what she thought no matter how radical or Buddhist. Her advice to write from our hearts sounded logical. I liked how what she said is full of common sense of the sort I learned from my parents. She assured us that what she offered in an evening talk during the retreat would be what she believed, and repeated we are not expected to become Buddhist. She told us frequently that we shouldn't believe anything she said but encouraged us to experience it for ourselves. I questioned whether this fearlessness and lack of concern for what the other thought would become part of my evolving definition of spirituality.

Nearly the oldest person in attendance, I wanted to speak freely without my usual hesitation and throat clearing. There was one woman older, but I judged that she was why people disliked elders as my feeling was that she talked too much. Now remembering the retreat with a psychoanalytic lens, I suspect that unconsciously I made a decision not to follow in her footsteps and voice an opinion on every subject. In hindsight, it appears that I went to the opposite extreme and most of the time I was with group members, I let intimidation take me by the throat and silence me. It also might have been my personalized Christian self that was giving me problems, the part of me afraid of letting go of Christian beliefs. My unconscious undoubtedly predicted some kind of trouble if I became too chummy with Buddhists. She asked the question of what was behind our desire to write, and I found myself courageously pushing past frogs in my throat and hoarsely replying that I want to write to help people go deeper. In response, Piver said, "To do this you have to be honest without being confessional." Confessional is a Catholic word in my book, and I am uncertain what she meant, but I was too shy to ask.

When it was time to depart from the retreat, I sensed in myself a degree of disappointment. These feelings came despite meaningful circumambulations around the inspiring stupa, delicious vegetarian food, gorgeous scenery, contemplative walks, deep meditation sessions, and connections with other group members who are writers. The disappointment centered around feeling I had not established a personal relationship with Susan. I imagined, again using my hard-earned psychoanalytic lens, that this desire to have a personal relationship with Susan was related to my longtime desire of being a colleague or friend of my analyst. Historically, I have needed to have a one-on-one relationship before a relationship has any importance to me. I am imagining this is because the dual nature of a couple replicates the first six years I spent as an only child with my mother.

I was full of awe when I witnessed Susan's courage and openness and felt a deep need to be her special friend. When she didn't know the answer to a question, she told us. Her heartfelt confession when she was feeling overwhelmed felt honest and not confessional, though I didn't fully understand the difference. It was obvious to me that her practice of generosity and enthusiastic effort, two of the six paramitas, a standard list of six character perfections she taught us, were important to her. She also knew how to drape a scarf dramatically around her throat in a manner that didn't hamper her expression.

After a while an old habit pattern, as the Buddhists might say, began surfacing. Because I had not been successful in establishing a close one-to-one relationship with Susan, I noticed myself concocting reasons to be critical of her. The urgency to find flaws to focus on rose within me. Using my psychoanalytic mind, I realized that I did not want to find fault with Susan in the manner my mother criticized other women. I wondered if my mother's relationships with other women had been hampered by a desire to be in closer relationship with them. Mom's usual accusation was that the other was shallow, a characteristic that I was terrified I might see and then be unable not to see in Susan, my meditation teacher and spiritual companion. Did Mom view her friends and relatives as shallow because of her own fears?

And now as I finish processing this extended memory of my time with Susan, I connect with an open, free feeling place I have been slowly discovering. I wonder if Mom really was critical of women in the way I thought she was or if it was me who felt hauntingly superior and projected it on my mother? I know it bodes well for my growth that I am engaging with these questions, but it is painful. As a longtime member of Susan Piver's Open Heart Project, I have the opportunity to observe how Susan develops and becomes more psychologically and spiritually mature and handles the pain that comes from transformation. I see her progress. My hope is that I am growing too. It feels I am making progress because I am able to appreciate my ability to observe her development even though I haven't been in the type of relationship with her that I prefer. The connection we have is different from my old, preferred way of being special, being the only one.

Later this year, when my memoir will be ready for

publication, I will tap into Susan's model of fearlessness and ask if she would read my memoir and write a blurb. I will be thrilled and honored when she agrees to my request. I am nearly incredulous when in her blurb, she writes that I had not conceived of psychoanalysis as merely a means of self-improvement. She knew before I did of how my spiritual leanings led me to and through analysis. She describes my experiences in psychoanalysis as a journey home through the discovery of trust—in self, in process, and in the innate wholeness of our world. Maybe, I decide, these words will be the basis of a new definition of spirituality.

Savoring this new sense of connection with Susan, I ponder reasons I did not pay much attention for years to my connection with the Open Heart Project. It had been such a different type of relationship than I was used to. I paid my monthly dues. I was one of many in the community. I didn't feel special. I wasn't totally connected to the Buddhist way of thinking. I kept hearing Susan use the word spiritual, and I kept wondering what the word might mean for me. At times I resorted to cynical thinking about how much money Susan was making from all of us. But after her generosity of offering to read my memoir and her prescient words of understanding my process, my thinking is changing. I am becoming more open to meeting different ways of thinking.

Early in the year I make a decision to sign up for a six-week class, *Buddhism in Modern Life*, offered by Susan's Open Heart Project. Before the first class on March 2, 2020, I start to wonder how Buddhism will fit with psychoanalysis. What will Freud and Buddha have in common? Noting on the Open Heart Project website that the instructor, Michael Carroll, recommends two books for the class, I wonder why, in spite of my previously biased belief that Buddhist literature is too simplistic, my mouth waters. I want to buy both books immediately. Instead, I take a firm stance with myself. I will not purchase them. I have too many books already. My refusal to purchase these much-wanted books feels like a noble act, one I actually pat myself on the back for making. I am growing up, I think to myself; I am finally facing reality, the type of reality I had become aware of in psychoanalysis. I righteously discern while deciding whether to purchase the books that I would not have time to read them if I did have them on my shelf. There is a bit of truth to this; it would mean giving up my psychoanalytic literature reading time, and I didn't feel ready to do that yet. I felt certain that my decision to not purchase these books was right for me.

In retrospect, the pride I felt in deciding not to purchase the two recommended Buddhist texts probably was misguided instead of virtuous. Now I can see that not purchasing them and making time to read them pointed toward my resistance to meeting in a deeper way another style of being in the world. Evidently my ego picked up on my spiritual yearning and saw this hunger as dangerous, fearing it was becoming too powerful, and put the kibosh on my desire.

Carroll, assuming that anyone who had signed up for this class would know Siddhartha as Buddha's birth name, opened the first session by announcing that we are in the same position as Siddhartha in the sixth century B.C.E. This proclamation surprised me. Carroll then explained for we humans, like Siddhartha, "something is off." This reminded me of a question my editor asked when working on my debut memoir, "Why exactly did you begin psychoanalysis?" and how difficult I found it to answer that question. Maybe I was led to analysis because something was off? In a strange way that made sense to me.

I was given a clue when Carroll said you can be endowed and still sense that something is off. I knew endowed was the perfect word to describe my condition; I had a home of my own, a reliable car, a vocation I loved, children and grandchildren who were healthy, tickets to the symphony. I was privileged as a white middle-class woman. But was I yearning for more aliveness, more depth of meaning? Carroll thought that even if we were endowed, when something was not going as planned or something was not working out to match our expectations, we have the feeling something is off. He added that you might say something was tickling us. He suggested that becoming conscious of unsatisfying feelings was an indication we were beginning to engage with the dilemma of being human. This was reassuring. I agreed with him that there was something disorienting about being alive. Little did I know that soon the disorientation he spoke of would ramp up and we would all be more awake and aware of the ordinary uncertainty life can offer.

To conclude the first class, Carroll issued the reminder, lest we forget, that life was disorienting. I thought about how Freud believed humans repressed this sense of disorientation. When Carroll spoke, we were unaware that in a few days, everyone's awareness of the ever present but normally hidden sense of disorientation would be placed on center stage. At the time he bid us farewell, no one knew how heightened our sense of disorientation would become. Dare I say, every inhabitant of the United States, not to mention people around the world, when learning about the coronavirus, felt a degree of disorientation. This was scary news. Nearly everyone talked about the pandemic. In Iowa, it has taken over as the number one subject of conversation replacing the weather. Comparisons with the Spanish Flu in 1918 begin to circulate. This is the same day, March 11, that I receive an email notice from a mail-order grocery service informing me that because of the coronavirus, they want me to know that orders are backed up and there are shortages of some products.

My initial reaction to this warning is panic—I want to order lots of food! I realize that if I did this, I would be hoarding, the type of behavior Buddhists criticize and one I observed in my mother. I remember how Mom had ample food crammed on the shelves behind the kitchen door that led to steps downstairs to the unfinished basement, food in the basement itself, and food in the freezer both at home and in the locker at the meat processing plant in our nearby small town. I had been critical and questioned why she chose to stockpile so much food but when I feel the fear of not being able to get what I need, I decide she may have acted out of fear, the fear I suddenly felt. I remember Mom's stories of living through the Depression. Would our situation become that serious? If she were alive, I would tell her I was sorry for my lack of understanding and critical judgmentalism. If only she were here. Suddenly I am experiencing the taste of being terrified; my breath uneven and hard to regulate. Me, who historically ate every few hours or when barely hungry, felt ungrounded; how would I survive if I didn't have enough food?

A few short days later, on Monday, March 16, 2020, I write in my daily journal that when I tell Wendell I am leaving for the analyst's office, he says somewhat jokingly, "Don't touch her," to which I reply, "It's more like don't breathe, isn't it?" I am trying to sort through all the information being offered by the news media on how to keep safe. Do I really have to wipe down everything I bring into the house with disinfectant? Lists of cancellations and closings take over the news media. Wendell assures me that we both will get sick with the virus. I don't want to get sick. I hope he is wrong. I do not want to die, which seems a very real possibility.

My analytical session on March 16 turns out to be the final time I will ever lie on the analyst's analytical couch even though I have eight months of the termination process ahead if I count March. Later, I think of how being on the couch for the last time fit into a category of things—those things that you don't know will never happen again when you are doing them for the last time. So much happens in twenty-four hours that on March 17, I write in my journal that I am too afraid to go out of the house for my session. I think of my mother as it is her St. Patrick's Day birthday. She would have been eight-six years old today. Even though I wish she were here, I am glad she doesn't have to go through this scary time. The analyst and I must have agreed to phone sessions the day before though I don't remember that conversation and didn't make note of it. I am in a minor state of shock the whole week.

In preparation for my phone session, I decide it would make sense to recline on the bed in the room where I usually sleep as that would be private and most resemble the analyst's office. Little did I know that this would be the analytical couch for the next eight months. As I write that, I want to double-check my numbers. Did we really have sessions on the phone for eight months? Yes, we did.

I prop my shoulders and head on my pillow, cover myself with a clean and cozy warm blanket that could have my name on it, and I am ready for my session. I gaze towards the foot of the bed and notice the beautiful purple batik that Jo, one of my best friends in the world, a New Zealand friend I met in India, shipped to me. When staring closely at the purple batik print, I note little circles with sticks poking out in a design similar to the images in the newspaper depicting the coronavirus. Days ago I had never heard of coronavirus and now I can't get away from it. On everyone's mind and heart, now depicted in my bedroom.

"Are you okay?" was my question after I select the ana-lyst's name from my list of contacts and push the little green box that features an old-fashioned phone receiver. I inquire this after brief hellos, thinking this an inquiry, considering the current circumstances, that would warrant a straight answer.

"Let's talk about that," she responds, "I hear worry in your voice."

"Yes, I am worried about you—I don't think that is unusual

considering the circumstances," I say, feeling more than a touch of irritation. Isn't it okay to voice my inner concerns about her?

"Since you couldn't see me, you didn't know if I was okay?" she inquires.

"I want you to stay safe," I say. In response, she stays silent. During this pause, I notice and then mention to her how I am feeling sad viewing Jo's lovely purple batik hanging on the wall and that it contains images scarily like the coronavirus. The analyst was a witness to an outpouring of grief from me when Jo died in 2014, so I think she will not be surprised to hear that when looking at the batik, I feel sad.

"You didn't expect Jo to die," Denae responds. Then she adds, "You didn't expect the virus."

I feel her comments are speaking directly to my habitual need to control and I agree that she has a point. I don't ask her what she means about my expectations or argue with her as I might have in the past. I figure that these two observations are interpretations, statements an analyst presents to an analysand to increase their level of awareness, or as my spiritual friends would say, level of consciousness. It is true I didn't think Jo would die—I mean, I knew Jo would die someday but not before I did, as she was younger. Jo was spiritual and I equate spirituality with longevity—this an unconscious belief I didn't know I had until after she died. When alive, Jo had connections with beings that I couldn't see and heard things I could not hear. In her emails, she shared long, drawn out descriptive stories about exploring various painful happenings in her past, how when confronting these events, she cried and screamed and then felt a sense of healing. I used to feel that Jo was doing what the analyst wanted me to do. Express feelings freely.

But if I remember Jo's stories correctly, she was usually the injured party. Her reports of healing came when she discerned she wasn't at fault. This felt disloyal to recall in this blaming way. Maybe I should recover some of her old emails to reread with my new eyes. In the process of working through my own painful experiences, the analyst has always confronted me, wondering what my part had been, as in what part was I was responsible for? Did Jo realize what her responsibility was? Oh, I wish she was still alive so I could write to her or call her about her view of spirituality and dialogue about the fears that were coming up for me. Was I remembering her stories correctly?

As this first session lying on my faux analytical couch, connecting with the analyst on the phone, draws to a close, I think to myself that the session had contained all the earmarks of a routine session held in her office. But I feel a bit of disappointment in both of us. I thought I had given up on my desire for her to be different some time ago, but it seems I am still wishing. Undoubtedly this was at the root of my irritation. I want her to be a colleague. And as for her, I had hope she could let go of her analytical attitude and just be a real person in this new crisis. I notice that as the session unfolds, my tendency to risk more, to say more of what I am feeling, is increasing. I know that partly this is because of the psychoanalytic theory my analyst continues to use; that even in the midst of a pandemic, she stays wedded to theory. We were not having social time just because there was a pandemic! Because she has discipline and I realize how helpful this has been for me, I feel compelled to continue my effort to understand the type of psychoanalytic theory she practices.

So, I keep looking everywhere I can think of to find information about Freud's psychoanalysis. I feel as if I hit the jackpot when I discover a podcast from the International Psychoanalytic Association with host Harvey Schwartz. Harvey interviews analysts all over the world on how they are coping with internal and external fears related to COVID-19. Listening to these podcasts helps me not feel so alone. The subject of one interview is tolerating uncertainty, which I am feeling quite frequently. Another interview proposes that we are dealing with two pandemics, with the first pandemic being the virus and the second, anxiety.

Hearing the words pandemic of anxiety encourages me to take stock of my situation since the diagnosis for my time in psychoanalysis was anxiety disorder. After a few deep breaths, I feel relieved that I don't feel all that anxious. Of course I am worried. I worry about my children and my grandchildren and my siblings and my friends. But I am not frantic. Today I wouldn't qualify for an anxiety disorder as described in the diagnostic manual. Because of the long stint in analysis healing my anxiety disorder, I know how to focus my mind and think about what is going on, to stay in reality despite the pandemic. I feel grateful. All the work I have done is paying off.

When I finally sign off from the psychoanalytic podcast, I blink my eyes a few times and wonder how long the pandemic will last. Will I continue to reap the rewards of my hard work? Will I meet with the virus or my previous anxiety?

6

Traveling/Attunement

April 2020

I experience my first psychoanalytic thought at the age of five. The occasion: April Fool's Day. At the time, of course, I wouldn't have used such a big word, a word Freud brought into being to describe his method of treating people with neurosis. Psychoanalytic thinking, a discovery I make lying on an analyst's couch, means looking below the surface, realizing the layers that appear behind words and actions. As a child, if I had known the meaning of this multi-syllable word psychoanalysis had something to do with pathology, I would have never considered it as a description of myself or my family; the people of my household were exemplars of mental health. My belief that no person in my family qualified for a diagnosis was rock solid.

My 1950s analytical thought related to an observation I make on the opening day of April; a day worthy of celebration in the household where I grew up. A shift in the relationship dynamics between my parents. Here's the backstory: on an average day, my parent's relationship was traditional in structure. Dad farmed to make the money, deciding where it was to be spent while Mom was responsible for feeding and clothing him and me. Mom remained adamant throughout my childhood that I would do nothing to upset my father. She, fearful of anger, didn't want any of it in our home. These gender roles, being the norm for our church and farm community, were not unusual in the 1950s. They were normal to me at the age of five and it would be many years before I questioned this arrangement of women being submissive to their husbands and, in addition, to God the Father.

On that first day of April it was a bit chilly, so when Mom whispered in my ear to meet her on the side porch, I hoped she wouldn't make us stay out there long because I was not dressed yet. I wondered if what she was going to tell me would relate to her big belly, which was fascinating to me because of how large it had become in the last several months. I knew the story about how Dad and I had convinced her to have another baby because Dad didn't want me to be an only child like he was. Our meeting on the porch wasn't about the pregnancy. When we were safely alone, she bent down and whispered in my ear, "Nicky, I put salt in the sugar bowl!" I grinned at her because I knew it was an April Fool's joke but as we snuck back into the kitchen, I felt a bit of worry as I took my seat at the breakfast table. How would Dad react? What if he got angry?

I was curious what would happen. What would his reaction be when he sipped his morning cup of Lipton tea, and it was salty? I lowered my eyes, so I was not staring directly at him. I didn't want to ruin Mom's joke because she seemed so happy about it. The moment his tongue tasted the salt, he sat up straight and his eyes popped open wide. When Mom saw this, she shouted, "April Fool!" They looked at each other and laughed. I experienced a sense of relief. For one thing, this meant the part of me that took responsibility for making sure they got along could relax. And I realized that I was a witness to Mom temporarily abandoning her subordinate role in the family. And the good news was that Dad didn't seem upset. Mom looked satisfied with herself. Her dark eyes shone with pleasure. She had put one over on him.

My mischievous side has always had a fascination with the idea of a harmless prank or hoax but this year, 2020, I am not planning to play any traditional practical jokes. Somehow it doesn't feel appropriate. We are dealing with too many surprises already. Pandemic continues to be the word on everyone's lips. This word, all over the newspapers, is soon known by the label COVID-19, which stands for Coronavirus Disease 2019. Each time I hear an estimate of how many people are ill with the virus, I shudder. My husband's prediction is that we will both contract the virus. This feels like a curse that runs through my mind frequently. I choose to limit my consumption of news. My new normal becomes more time than usual on social media. I am home all the time except for my walks. Being on the computer is my attempt to escape feeling lonely in a sequestered existence that is now becoming routine. The internet is my connection to others. I enroll in writing classes offered by the International Women's Writing League. I appreciate the diversity of offerings, most of which I am not interested in at this stage of my writing life, but I am relieved to know there is still activity in the world.

I register for and attend one Zen virtual half-day retreat. Initially, I cannot imagine meditating in a Zoom room, but that is the only option for this retreat. My days of traveling across the street to the Pure Land Temple for these retreats are now precious memories. I have been practicing Zen meditation off and on since the late 1980s, but never thought of it as particularly spiritual. It was a secular endeavor in my mind and this memory reminds me of the strict separation I have been keeping between the sacred and the secular.

For the most part, I feel good about how I am attuning to the uncertainties of the pandemic. I am sleeping fairly well and keeping up with my household duties. Yet on Good Friday, April 10, 2020, my unconscious indicates I have been ignoring my bruised feelings. The unacceptable happens: I space off my regular 9:00 AM Friday appointment with the analyst. I don't call her. I don't even think about calling her. Our sessions on Friday at 9:00 AM have been on my schedule for years. But nonetheless, I forget. In my journal I note that her response to my forgetting is to call me at ten minutes after the hour. When I hear her voice, I blurt out, "I've never forgotten before"—most likely an attempt to defend myself. "That's why I called," she replies. I note that in the journal entry, I add quotation marks around "forgot" because apparently I deduce my forgetting is not an error without cause. At the time, my unconscious kept mute on motivation.

A phrase familiar to any Freudian psychoanalytic lover came to mind while musing on forgetting my appointment: the past is in the present. In this case, the trigger that led to the past being present took place in the previous Wednesday phone session when Denae practically shouts: "I am hearing an annoying scratching sound."

When she says that, I reply breezily, "Doing nothing different here so don't know what it is." After making this crystal clear to the analyst by utilizing a detached tone of voice, inwardly I reassure myself, *this is not my problem.*

"Where is the microphone on your earbuds?" Denae continues, using an authoritative tone, her voice having an edgy sound, a bit provocative, I think. I wouldn't go as far as saying snarky, but definitely unapologetic.

"I have no microphone on my earbuds," I respond assuredly, maintaining and defending my not guilty position.

"Would you look and see because I am pretty certain that

you have one and that you are brushing against it to make the distraction." There was not a hint of sympathetic expression in her tone.

I am incredulous. There is NO microphone on my cheap set of earbuds. I continue to hotly deny doing anything that would cause the scratchy sound. I repeat to myself that it is not my fault she is having problems. It is embarrassing to recall my ignorance being so out there in front! But I had been certain. Amidst all the pandemic uncertainties, I was sure about not causing obnoxious noise for my analyst.

It hurt me she was thinking I would purposefully make our call uncomfortable for her. Of course, I don't admit the hurt her tone of voice inflicts on me, but in my usual fashion, have chosen to bury my feelings. My unconscious, knowing there is unfinished business, arranges for me to miss an appointment. I forget an appointment! During a later session while discussing the possible location of my microphone (I never did really locate it) she admits to making her complaint in a more forceful manner than usual. It was embarrassing to admit even to myself that my "forgetting" was a way of getting back at her, but I feel certain it was. Freud's prime discovery is that's how the unconscious works. The lesson for me is to note—keep conscious—when I feel the soft wisps of hurt and then express them in a non-blaming way. Analysis on the phone is proving to be effective.

Between sessions, I begin musing about differences between Freud and Jung. This question has arisen because of registering for an online workshop later in the month led by Susan Tiberghien. Susan is a Jungian analyst, and I am curious about her decision to choose Jung over Freud. Since March is a long month and I have time on my hands, I decide to investigate more fully the differences between Freud and Jung and find the reasons for their split. Initially, I find they are very different men. Freud grew up in poverty and his interests focused on conventional success, money, fame, and reputation.

Jung grew up in a village in Switzerland as the only son of a country pastor and his mystical wife until he was nine years old.

I just keep finding more information on each of these men. Freud was nineteen years older than Jung. Jung read Freud's work and thought of him as a brilliant older man, an ideal father with whom he could talk openly about all his inner states and emotions. The correspondence between them was instigated by Jung, to which Freud eagerly responds. Freud and Jung share a strong bond of disdain for people who criticize psychoanalysis. As their relationship develops, Jung discloses to Freud his "religious crush" on his older colleague (Whitebook, 2017).

Freud's initial hypothesis on the theory and existence of the unconscious was met with people's denial, many choosing to refute the possibility of an unconscious. Most people were largely unable to comprehend what he was proposing. We now know that Freud was assigning a name to an experience widely shared, a feeling that we often act in ways we experience as outside of our control (Frosh, 2006). Jung initially agreed with Freud's ideas about the unconscious but later began to disagree with him. Jung believed Freud placed too much emphasis on sexuality. Jung's concern was more for the salvation of the community, not the analysis of the individual (Schwartz, 2020). Freud was a secular Jew and Jung a Christian.

The more information I gather, the more interesting the relationship between Freud and Jung becomes. I begin to feel connections with both men. Tiberghien's upcoming online workshop becomes even more enticing. Her memoir, *Looking for Gold: A Year in Jungian Analysis*, is the first memoir I read where the analytic process is described in detail. While reading about her process of being in analysis, I ignore her allegiance to Jung.

"By way of introduction," the first section in her book, discloses how her book came into being as the result of an early morning dream, a dream which lays out for her the book's title and outlines the book's complete structure. This rekindles my longtime desire to pay attention to my dreams. What I most appreciate learning is when her friends hear she is going into analysis, they ask what is wrong with her. They wonder if she is unhappy with herself or her family or her writing. I cheer when she informs them she doesn't think there is anything wrong with her but explains she is searching for something deeper.

I resonate with her words, *wanting more depth.* Apparently by calling attention to and attaching importance to these words, my unconscious is informing me: my desire had been for more depth in my life. Tiberghien describes to her friends how she thinks that the soul is part of analysis, soul being a word I have long associated with Jung. I would thankfully discover during my research that Freud also used the word soul, but translators, when putting Freud's words into English, wrongly translate the word soul to words more abstract, depersonalized, highly theoretical. They attempt to use words that make Freud's work sound more scientific and, according to Bruno Bettelheim, these inaccurately translated words detract from describing Freud's deep feeling for what is most human in all of us (Bettelheim, 1982).

I am vague when finally I disclose to my friends that I am in Freudian psychoanalysis. Articulating the reasons I was drawn to analysis didn't come easy like it had for Tiberghien. I wonder anew how it will be to participate in a workshop with her. Fast forward through the month, and the verdict is her workshop is a delight. It is not a surprise when she is gentle and very wise. The workshop is an hour and a half that I am not thinking about COVID-19.

I like working with Tiberghien, so I order her other book,

Writing Toward Wholeness. Feelings of disloyalty to Freud arise when this book arrives in the mail, and I note the subtitle: *Lessons Inspired by C. G. Jung.* I try to focus on the main title: *Writing Toward Wholeness.* I feel inspiration when I read the promise made on the cover: this type of writing will help weave a fabric of psyche that includes conscious and unconscious material. That's where the wholeness in the title comes in, I speculate. I feel reassurance when Freud is mentioned in her text as helping with the exploration of the psyche through his writing. Tiberghien makes it appear possible that I, too, can go inward and find my soul. I feel excitement about the book and want to work on the exercises she proposes, but the book ends up on my pile of books to be read. Soon forgotten is the excitement generated on the first day. I return to reading about Freud's psychoanalytic theory where I focus on the theories my analyst uses.

In addition to exploring the differences between Freud and Jung, I begin thinking about the word spiritual and what it means to me. I feel my old strictly Christian definition (that to be spiritual is to believe in God and His son Jesus) uses language that is too narrow and no longer expresses the layers and depth I am tuning in to. I have begun thinking of Buddhist literature with the focus on loving-kindness and compassion as spiritual. Comfort is important to me and I notice that I feel safe when paying attention to my breath as I do with Susan Piver's Open Heart Project and Zen meditation. My definition of spirituality is burgeoning.

Eventually I become familiar with the wide range of Buddhist groups, each with a different focus. I haphazardly draw a division between groups that focus on wisdom in combination with the study of ancient and modern texts (which largely translates as sitting or walking meditation while following one's breath) and other groups that concentrate on compassion. In actuality, I am not very clear that I have made this distinction. During an intimate discussion taking place after a Dharma talk during a Zen retreat, a man young enough to be my grandson speaks up. He says that what he heard me say and confidently shares with all in the circle is that I appear more comfortable with wisdom as a focus more than compassion. Initially, I bristle at his observation because I see myself as a loving person and I conflate compassion and love. Learning the language of Buddhism is challenging.

As the month of April draws to a close, I decide to forgive myself for 'forgetting' the Good Friday analytical appointment. Since my adoption of a psychoanalytic perspective helps makes clear reasons behind my forgetfulness, it is delightful when self-forgiveness comes easier than usual. This is a delicious experience, a taste of maturity. I smile. I am still smiling when on a Sunday afternoon, I carve out time for contemplation and I am visited by the poignant memory of a visit several years ago with my maternal grandmother on Good Friday. I bravely drove my car to visit her in the nursing home, a town I had never driven to before. I say bravely because it is a challenge for me to drive to locations I have never visited before since my sense of direction is faulty and I confuse left and right frequently. But my desire was great, I needed to see her, so I filled up the gas tank and headed off.

"Little Gram" smiled widely as I approached her and appeared to respond positively to my offer for an outdoor walk. As we neared the threshold, Little Gram (her nickname as she was shorter than any of her grandchildren) jerked her arms out stiffly, her hands reaching out to clutch the door frame. Her small round face, circled with the gray hair we share, revealed feelings of panic and fear. Wheelchair bound, shrunken from osteoporosis, she prevented us from going any further. Her actions mimicked my own fear of travel. Like her, I always felt enthusiastic when thinking and preparing for a journey until time to leave. At departure time, I have felt a dull ache inching up my neck toward the crown of my head. This is a sign that my anxiety has been triggered. Thankfully, convincing Little Gram to release the grip on the door frame wasn't difficult, as she only needed my calm reassurance. Since similar feelings of fear were familiar to me, it was easy to squat beside the wheelchair and reassure her.

It was warm for early in the season, and we leisurely made our way down a paved trail. After a few minutes, I pulled us off the path so we could celebrate being together. Now she was peaceful. When I knelt down on the grass and put my head on her lap, she gently stroked my hair. It occurred to me as I soaked in the love we shared that she trusted me and had forgotten her fear. Her gentleness brought tears to my eyes. I use this memory as a way to conquer the fear I have of not surviving the pandemic. I am afraid. Despite the pandemic fears, my spiritual side is more active. Remembering my grandmother is helping me reconnect to spiritual roots. Little Gram attended church services and read the Bible. She was a religious woman who had faith and a healthy intellect. I don't know if she ever had doubts about God or religion.

I have doubts and it might be accurate to say that after reconnection with my high school sweetheart in 2009, eleven years prior to the pandemic, I had begun to wrestle with a growing temptation to discard the entire spiritual arena because of the fear that dabbling in spirituality would likely be an obstacle on the analytic path. While in analysis, there seemed no place for this spiritual part of me, so I let anything that spoke of the sacred take a back seat. I held a great deal of respect for Freud's creation of psychoanalysis and had learned so much about reality that I had trouble knowing how to fit the sacred in without being disloyal to the theory that had given me this new life. I still distrust Jung's theory. After all my analytical work, I am cautious. I am not about to be fooled into believing things that are not true. But I am considering the word spiritual in new ways, which feels promising, ways that won't require me to sacrifice my intellect. If I add any magic to my life, I am resolute it will not deny reality. What else will change as I deal with the pandemic?

75

7

Totems

May 2020

My Moleskine journal entries for May 2020 feature pages of beautiful abstract squiggles created using a black felt-tipped Pentel marker, a marker highly recommended by Austin Kleon, a writer who draws. In my mind, Kleon's doodles qualify as works of art, at least in comparison to my beginner doodles. Kleon's testimonial for Pentel made more sense after I viewed his descriptive, eye-catching, humorous sketches online. Once in a while I have noticed myself fantasizing our sketches are totems for creativity. Totem, an old-fashioned word, referring to symbols that hold spiritual significance, was added to my lexicon in 2018 after participating in a Shamanic workshop offered at Wangapeka Retreat Centre, New Zealand. Kleon knows nothing of my totem label for his work; I've felt shy about contacting him because he appears to be busy with his children. I am always impressed when I read his sign-off to weekly messages of the ten things he thought worthwhile to mention that week, where he writes his newsletters are free, but they are not cheap. If given an opportunity to speak to Kleon, I would tell him how much I appreciate his attitude that free doesn't imply cheap and then share with him that I have adopted a similar attitude about the blog, Instagram, and FB posts I've shared on social media. The posts are free but not cheap, unlike some expensive items that support my creativity.

Moleskin notebooks are not cheap, but I have selected their thick, creamy, smooth paper as the recipient of my daily journal entries for many years, justifying the expenditure by conscientiously filling every page. It has become a ritual that when I make the last dated entry, the journal is ceremoniously closed, and is magically transformed into a totem, a symbol of my ever-evolving self-reflection. I have venerated a ten-and-a-half-inch stack of filled-to-the-brim soft-covered black notebooks stashed near my left knee in a desk cubbyhole for many years. These are prized possessions, filled with intimate details. In retrospect, when I have reviewed the entries, a significant percentage of them appear to be an amplification of the ordinary events in my life. Dysfunctional times when I reacted instead of responding.

A journal entry dated the first day of May noted that instead of going across a gravel road delivering violet-filled May baskets, I prepared for the first analytical session of the month. While preparing my at-home faux analytical couch by smoothing the purple velvet duvet cover, removing lumps that might disturb my ability to free associate, I experienced an epiphany. This sudden rush of knowing, explaining in a new fashion my connection to the analyst, initially felt strangely spiritual in nature. However, I quickly pushed any sacred implications out of my awareness. I had not yet prepared myself to recognize and honor thoughts that I had not manufactured myself. This thought recognized transference as part of my relationship with the analyst and came to my awareness entirely on its own. This type of knowing, a spontaneous thought given freely to me, I had not yet cultivated the mental discipline to accept.

It has been ten days since May Day, which means it was a day before my sister Nina's birth sixty-nine years ago. In my life, her birth has always qualified as an epiphany, but this was not the epiphany I was excited about telling the analyst. I will just mention that foremost in my unconscious mind was the realization that I had forever forfeited my exclusive relationship with my mother. The present day epiphany that I was eager to share with the psychoanalyst did not relate to the disappointment I felt with a new sibling. This present day epiphany was a new realization that the way I related to the analyst was comparable to how I traditionally had related with my parents. This felt spiritual because it arrived in the form of an epiphany; it had been a gift, not something I had created. I felt this knowing qualified as a psychological truth because it had a degree of complexity, and I needed help to unpack all the layers and I felt confident the analyst could help me.

I wanted to integrate the concept of transference. A well-known narrative is about Freud's early concern that when a patient responded to the analyst in the same manner as they related to their parents, it was a problem. I wonder how long it took Freud to come to this conclusion? When I hear this story, I think how clever Freud was not clinging to his disappointment therefore letting it stop him from continuing his research.

At the same time, this eureka moment of deciphering the cause of my at times troublesome relationship with the analyst appeared as obvious as the kitchen sink; so embarrassingly simple! Not at all sophisticated. There wasn't a particular incident that had clued me in, but since the insight came in the form of an epiphany, there didn't have to be a recognizable cause. I just knew that to me, this knowing was shockingly apparent: I tried to please the analyst in the same manner I had tried to please my parents. I was again giving up my sense of self to garner approval. This, of course, was simply an example of transference, a behavior well known in Freud's world. As I continued to get ready for the phone call to Denae that would initiate our first session of the month and my disclosure, I walked across the bedroom to shut the bedroom door. I wanted more privacy.

The epiphany continued to unfold, much to my wry amusement, and took on more meaning as I passed a full-length mirror on my way to the door. I giggled as I realized that when I applied psychoanalytic attention to glancing at myself in the mirror, I discerned that the analyst functioned like a mirror when she reflected my patterns back to me. I judged my discovery sophisticated and feeling secure and ready, I lowered my body to a horizontal position for the session. I mused to myself that every person I knew acted as a mirror! I was so excited with these new knowings—of course, neither was totally new, but both were new in the way I integrated them in my psyche. My entire body could feel the knowing. I was on to something important!

With these neonate knowings on my tongue, I stretched out on the bed that was pretending to be an analytical couch. Arranging my pillows as I reclined, I pushed the green button on my cell phone to connect with the analyst. After we both acknowledged the other's presence, without any hint of small talk which would mislead me about the nature of the analytic experience by offering reassurances that would calm my anxiety, I, without hesitation, launched into an explanation of my newborn epiphanies. I told her, probably with an excess of emotion that at the time felt essential and was mostly sourced by my unconscious, about the realization that I had been treating her in the same manner as I had interacted with my parents. Then without taking time for a breath, I continued to tell her how she and everyone I knew acted as mirrors. I heard myself explain my insights several different ways. The realization that I had expected her to gasp at my brilliance and appoint me her star analysand didn't become conscious until she said:

"If you clean up what you project on me, you lose a way to learn about yourself."

I was taken off guard by her response, but when I took a deep breath, I discovered that I wasn't totally surprised. I started imagining that if I hadn't burst out first thing, if I had thought about it longer, I could have changed my presentation of these so-called epiphanies and she would have responded differently. Perhaps with more thought, I could have garnered a different response. Or maybe if I hadn't been quite so exuberant, so sure of myself, it would have been different. If I had used my hard-earned knowledge from years of analysis, I might have concluded that while these were not exactly secret epiphanies I was going to hide from her, they were gems I could keep locked away in the privacy of my mind. It could have been knowledge for me to savor and celebrate. She probably assumed that I knew all this—and I did—but not in my new full-bodied manner.

I continued berating myself. If I had had the mettle to perform any of those actions, it might have prevented the rapid drop in mood when I heard her response. Hearing what I thought was a spot-on interpretation, I realized how deep my desire had always been for her to express admiration for my insights. Initially I was tempted to reenact my habitual response and fight her. Make a case for Freud's repetition compulsion. Reject her words. Tell myself she was the enemy and didn't understand me. I argued briefly with her about the correctness of her words but since I had understood and largely agreed with what she said, I tripped over my own words and soon came to the realization that she was more correct than I had initially believed. By bragging about my discoveries, I had been reverting to my old stance of being above it all. Or another way to verbalize her accuracy using her words: if I didn't project onto her the patterns from my past, she wouldn't be able to help me understand the forms in which my behavior unfolded and help me find ways to do it differently.

Trying to be humble, mostly succeeding, I informed her that I understood now how I was trying to avoid the work that an analysand needed to do to transform. This time, she agreed with me. Her simple reply to my confession, "yes." She didn't say more.

But the session wasn't over yet, and I kept ruminating. Since I was not totally clear on what type of suffering I was trying to avoid, I thought about asking, "What's the problem with that? Why is it a problem to avoid the struggle?" But since I had been in analysis for so long, I didn't directly ask her. I sat with the question for some time—or I should say I stayed on the analytical couch that was currently a bed and pondered what the answer might be. It didn't take me long to discern exactly what I was trying to avoid: Suffering. We talked for a bit about the fact that I am human and if I am human, there is no way to get out of suffering.

Of course when I say "we talked" I don't mean it was a normal conversation. It is more like I talked, there were pauses and silence and then occasionally she offered a word or two. This was an analytical conversation—the unique type of collaboration that I had learned so much from during my sessions with her. I was secretly beginning to worry about losing this type of communication in my life, especially when I kept recalling that we were in the termination process. I was beginning to feel the preparatory grief of losing these interactions. I was worried about suffering, but I wasn't clear with her about any of that. The session over, I disconnected the connection feeling deflated.

Michael Eigen comforted me when he proposed that a tantalizing trait of human nature is the ability to exaggerate in an effort to convey the truth of emotional experience (Eigen, Eigen in Seoul: Volume One, Madness and Murder, 2010). It is good to know that my embellishments are in service of expressing the real meaning of my emotions. Eigen is a psychoanalyst, so undoubtedly he has witnessed dramas in his office. Incorporating Eigen's insight that exaggerated emotional outbursts are a human trait has lessened my critical and judgmental ravings when I observe myself engaged in dramatic outbursts. I haven't found where Eigen discloses that another tantalizing trait of human nature is to create totems in service of symbolizing what is meaningful. I am only in volume one of his three volume work of transcribed lectures presented in Korea and have hope I may yet discover him mentioning totems.

I thought my dedication to journaling had been unwavering, but when I perused the actual notes in my journal for this session in order to write about it, the notes failed to capture what had occurred. All that was written on the page: "She said something important, and I heard her telling me to do it." I know that she would have never told me what to do; however, this serves as evidence of my deeply held wish for there to be one person that I could trust to have all the answers and that they would tell me what the right thing to do was.

In another session, I foolishly asked her what she was telling me to do. Her reply: "I'm not telling you to do anything. I'm just telling you what you do, do."

This struck me as a Freudian slip bordering on comedy and I respond by giggling: "It's hard not to comment on dodo." "Why?" she asked. "Because it is reminding me of third grade bathroom humor," I replied. "You don't want to be younger," she retorted, to which I spat back defensively, "I don't want to be immature or appear unsophisticated or gullible."

Regardless of what she implied when she suggested I didn't want to be younger, I knew that even if she had consented to tell me what to do, I would have rebelled against it or argued with her. This is the immaturity I was referring to, the naivety I feared was still present. Freud didn't write about the repetition compulsion for no reason. When the termination from analysis was complete, would I repeat my patterns unconsciously? Undoubtedly, this is what she had picked up on because my rebellion was not new. A prime example: One time during the middle part of our work together, I earnestly asked her to recommend a psychoanalytic book. I thought it a legitimate request, but her answer painted another picture: "I don't think you should read about psychoanalysis; I think you should experience psychoanalysis."

Those probably were not her exact words, but they are close. I think this is close to what she said even though what I proceeded to hear and put into practice was: "I forbid you to read psychoanalytic books!" One time I told her that this is how I had translated her answer to my request for a book. She paused and asked (if I could have seen her, I bet I would have seen a grin), "And then what did you do?" I knew it was a rhetorical question, but to humor her and because I was certain she was laughing with me and not at me, I responded, "I read all the damn psychoanalytic books I could get my hands on!" We both laughed heartily. It was this type of togetherness that I craved. I enjoyed this moment immensely and will never forget how poking fun at my immaturity brought me closer to the togetherness I craved. Every interaction fostered learning on my part.

During my analysis, I integrated the importance of developing intimate connections with significant others and an ability to know myself as a separate individual. As a result, I became conscious that I am responsible for my own life when I take part in relationships, that blaming others no longer made sense. The analyst did everything in her power to encourage me think for myself and be accountable for my own decisions. She would not answer my direct questions, which at times must have been frustrating for her as well because I kept pestering her. Her silence and lack of response forced me to formulate my own opinions. According to many biographies I consulted, Freud also struggled to become a separate self and admitted freely that in his self-analysis, the task of becoming his own person was a difficult endeavor. Freud was clear that while psychoanalytic theory could be counted on to enlighten people about the process of separation that led to a separate self, it could not make this an easy process.

One of the many books I gathered around me in an effort to understand the psychoanalytic theory that made my psychoanalyst so effective as an analyst was *Desire and the Political Unconscious in American Literature* by Sam B. Girgus (Girgus, 1990). There are many reasons I chose this particular book from the thousands available. Foremost, it was because it contained the word unconscious; I wanted to delve deeply into how Girgus used this word. Was Freud the only one who understood what this other layer of our minds consisted of?

I was intrigued by the reference to literature in the title. What place would literature have in my life now that I was thinking of myself as a writer? I believed my writer friends were literary. I knew Freud was well versed in classic literature; and that he thought literature could be read like dreams, that author's words related to their unconscious desires and fears. That's why when I am using a psychoanalytic lens, my reading has to have depth and layers of meaning.

I am curious how writers think about the unconscious and what it means to them, so the book by Girgus moved to the top of my stack. Girgus adopted a mature manner (at least from my perspective as an analysand) when he proposed that the therapeutic goal of psychoanalysis is to sever the umbilical cord of authority. I appreciated his using biological terms to describe a psychological issue; this was deemed sophisticated by me and thus literary but understandable. Girgus wrote that this severing of authority had to take place in order for there to be true love between two persons. The idea that psychoanalysis helps people gain autonomy certainly was my experience. During the years I was in psychoanalysis, this became an important objective in my process because I was raised in what family therapists have labeled an enmeshed family system, a system where autonomy is commonly thwarted to foster togetherness.

I tried to read Girgus's book with an analytical mind. Girgus indicated that while Freud had ridiculed Americans, he thought Freud should have recognized that democracy was a way of institutionalizing the Oedipus complex. Girgus was referring to the Oedipus complex, which was at the heart of Freud's work. Many of us know the story of how Oedipus killed a man that he didn't know was his father. The Oedipus complex that Freud created tells the story of replacing fathers with sons, which Girgus writes is what America's new democracy was designed to do. The transitional leader of this democratic process was George Washington, who Girgus perceives a kind of national totem.

My eyes stopped scrolling the text when I came across the word totem. As I mentioned earlier, my experience at a Shamanic workshop had elevated the word totem in my vocabulary. When I approached a meaningful object or person, I had begun labeling them as totems. I thought this way of thinking corresponded with Girgus citing Washington as a symbol of democracy. But I had an inkling there was more to learn about this old-fashioned sounding word, totem. It is an important word in the Shamanic world, so I pulled out my books on Shamanism. I am pleased that I followed subtle encouragement from my unconscious and kept nosing around.

I learned in *The Celtic Shaman: A Handbook*, written by John Matthews (Matthews, 1991) that shamanistic traditions teach we are born with innate gifts, talents such as being good with languages, music, or drawing. Many shamanistic traditions believe we are born with an attached spirit being which is sometimes called a totem beast. Matthews writes that this totem beast has the same quality of existence that many children experience when interacting with their invisible friends. Reading the words invisible friends brought tears to my eyes. I marveled at the depth of feeling provoked in me when I read Matthew's proposition about the similarities between how we experience relating with invisible friends and how we relate with a totem beast. The intensity of my feeling is unquestionably because I have experienced this type of relationship in the past. I do not remember my invisible friends but know they were so present to me that Mom made place settings for CheeChee and Mocha at our kitchen table.

Now that Matthew's work had given me a more inclusive definition of totem, my desire was to develop a relationship with my own totem. As I gazed at the portrait of Freud above my monitor, I wondered if he could fill the role. Freud became an important person in my life because of my experience in psychoanalysis but I didn't feel satisfied when I thought of him as a totem. I had resonated with Girgus's idea that Washington was a totem for democracy, so it wasn't that Freud was a person. But he was a man. Feminist that I am, I wanted my totem to have feminine qualities. I was clear that I wanted a totem. Hanging on the wall to the left of Freud's portrait is a drawing by Jenny Hahn that was part of her transformational series. I met Jenny when she presented for a Buddhist group I attend on Zoom.

During her presentation, Jenny showcased her drawings and mentioned they would be for sale on her website. I instantly fell in love with one work that featured an abstract tree that morphed into a woman holding the sun. I had to have it! But when I went to the website, I didn't find it. When I emailed her to inquire, she knew right away which painting I was referring to but told me it was not yet for sale. She explained that it was the first one she had drawn when she started her own transformational process, and it was so personal that she hadn't been clear whether or not she would offer it. She was pleased that I liked it and said she would load it onto the site, as she wanted me to have it. Along with my journals, it is now my prized possessions, one that while not my special totem, eventually guided me to choose my personal totem.

As I continued to think about possibilities for a meaningful totem, I again looked at Freud above my monitor. No, he's not my totem. That was clear. Then I glanced at Jenny's painting hanging beside it. It was so feminine, so many curvy lines and evocative images—circles, ovals, eyes. I loved looking at it and then I started wondering, what woman would I want for my feminist totem? Suddenly Christine Downing's name popped into my mind. I began to feel quite happy as I had acquired several of her books and resonated with her story. I remembered how her feminist friends, delighted when she was installed as the first female president of the American Academy of Religion in 1974, were dismayed, some were outraged, when she chose Sigmund Freud as the subject of her presidential address. Now there's a possible totem!

I pulled her books off my shelf and ordered a couple of used copies of other books I didn't have so I could see if she was still a fan of Freud's. I cheered when in a 2004 copyright book of hers, Downing disclosed that she was going to once again honor Freud with a speech, while at the same time, celebrate the one-hundredth anniversary of the publication of Freud's *Interpretation of Dreams*. Now my task was to learn what Downing appreciated about Freud and see if her ideas about Freud matched with those I had begun gathering. In other words, I was asking myself, would she be a good totem?

Downing acknowledged that there are many ways of reading Freud. Her way is a depth reading that could be considered a political reading, a poetic, or mythic reading (Downing, Preludes: Essays on the Ludic Imagination, 1961-1981, 2005). To me that means Freud can be seen as a therapist or a theorist, a scientist or a poet, or a realist or a romantic. Downing writes that to read Freud is to feel the tensions between those different ways of describing him. She believes that we learn from Freud by wrestling with his work. That his work cannot be reduced to meaning one thing, one interpretation. The more I learn about Downing, the more I am convinced that she can act as a totem for me. I will keep learning about her. What will her presence as my totem offer as the months of termination continue to wind down?

8

THE INNER SHAMAN

June 2020

When I turned the calendar page from May to June, I comprehended inwardly with a sense of immediacy that only four
months remained in the yearlong termination process. Admitting this awareness was not an entirely unpleasant feeling despite the fact that historically I have struggled to let go of a
marriage, relationships I've had with groups, old purses, out-
dated mascara, anything that once I was connected to or
owned. I knew that separation from the analyst and ending
the process of psychoanalysis would be a huge letting go. The
ease I felt was undoubtedly the increasing degree of connection I experienced towards my inner shaman. I felt good about
myself when I heard the new words that inhabited my vocabulary—inner shaman and totem. These particular words were
beginning to feel part and essential to the language I was
evolving to describe the spiritual world.

Reading Christine Downing's language, who last month I

officially designated as my totem, I am nourished. When she recognized the importance of honoring the tensions and contradictions in Freud's work, I felt excited. This, she wrote, was where she found the juice, the meaning (Downing 1977). Her rereading of Freud, she asserted, was because his language helped her find meaning. The idea of finding meaning reminded me of my experience being in analysis where the analyst helped me go below the surface, beyond the conscious level, so the meaning could be found to explain my life experience. In addition, reading tomes of psychoanalytic literature in addition to Downing's work led me to language that described my experience.

Perhaps this will be one of the functions of a totem: to challenge me to stay with the tension between the sacred and the secular or determine how they overlap or merge and find language to express my experience. Deep in the termination phase, I am becoming clearer that psychoanalysis, with Freud's insistence on free association as a technique which is anti-intellectual at its core but leads to pondering the unseen, has its own sense of the sacred. I remember hearing that Freud wanted psychoanalysis to replace religion. Freud knew that humans have always had the inherent desire for the spiritual linked with a desire to find meaning.

I thought I knew quite a bit about the sacred or what I called the spiritual part of life when I began my analysis with a Freudian psychoanalyst in 2007. I was spiritual because of my involvement in the United Methodist Church. I soaked up the sacred when I was a child in Sunday school, teenager in Methodist Youth Fellowship, young woman attending chapel at Morningside College, organizer of a Young Mother's group that met in the classroom at the church, and wife of a lay church administrator surrounded by clergy members. I realized now as I was moving closer to the final psychoanalytic session that what I had historically labeled spiritual or sacred was religion.

Growing up, I had been taught in Sunday School that I was a sinner and because I was a sinner, needed forgiveness of the sort granted by God the Father in order to have a chance at a decent afterlife. As an adolescent, I learned that God sent his son Jesus to die for my sins which made little sense to me though I tried to believe that it was true, especially when the Easter season rolled around. During Lent, it became quite evident we humans needed saving because we had betrayed Jesus and then killed him in a brutal way, all of which made it even more evident that we were sinners.

The idea that I was inherently good was a teaching I kept hearing once I started hanging around Buddhists. I attended extended retreats in order to learn how to meditate and eat slowly using frustrating Oryoki bowls where you are forced to eat everything you are given and then drink the water that cleans all the bowls. This felt to me like drinking dishwater. Everyone else appeared to take this dreadful state of affairs in stride so I chose not to complain lest that prove that I did not, after all, have as much inner goodness as was needed to be a true Buddhist. The idea of my essential goodness was also presented when I attended a Shamanistic retreat and then began to read shamanic literature. I was fascinated that Shamanism was older than Buddhism and both Shamanism and Buddhism were older than Christianity. I knew that Freud was Jewish, and that Judaism was older than Christianity. Perhaps being the oldest daughter of an oldest daughter gave credibility to those who came first. I realized this was an unconscious judgement, but it felt like truth to me.

I liked this idea of basic goodness and had experienced it when I cradled my three infant sons in my arms. I often observed from the sidelines how people were trying to express love as they interacted with others. Many people were kind. I was trying to find goodness in myself. In my reading, the idea that people had an inner shaman was presented, and I began to toy with the idea that this could also be true for me. In my mind, the inner shaman was the goodness of which the Buddhists spoke. After attending the shamanistic retreat, I started reading both Buddhist and Shamanistic literature in addition to psychoanalytic works.

When I discovered that a focus in Shamanism was on discovering how humans are related to all created beings, I was reminded of growing up on the farm. I loved being outdoors with my dog Yippy, swinging in Dad's Navy hammock between two huge oak trees, walking alone down the gravel road, playing in the weed-infested chicken yard with the solid, ancient-looking trees witnessing my play. The more I learned about Shamanism, the more I believed that unbeknowst to me, I had touched unconsciously into shamanistic teachings as a child. Of course, I didn't have words for any of this growing up, it was just a natural way of being a girl in the world. Nature provided a sense of the sacred for me.

Despite how evident all this appeared to my thinking mind, it took me a long time to take seriously my own inner shaman. When I remembered that a desire for the spiritual part of life had always been buried deep in my unconscious, I didn't share that with the analyst as I didn't have words to express this part of me and I remained committed to being sophisticated. I would need to find words before I shared this part of me with the analyst. Maybe the inner shaman was a way I could integrate the new spiritual knowing that was bubbling up inside me. Contemplating all this, I thought that dreams might be a connecting link between Buddhism, Shamanism, and Freudian psychoanalysis. This insight felt discouraging as I didn't feel comfortable with dreams, was getting ready to leave psychoanalysis, knew little about Shamanism, and was learning that Buddhism had so many branches that I could study it forever and not know it completely. I wondered if I could develop a big enough container to hold it all. Thinking about Christine Downing as my totem gave me confidence. She had a long career as professor and chair in the Department of Religious Studies at San Diego State University and in my mind, that gave her credibility. This musing led to speculation that maybe a dream would help me learn about my inner shaman.

As if in answer to my wish, I had a dream in the middle of June that I dutifully wrote in my journal. I was impressed by its clarity and wanted my analyst help to decipher its deeper meaning. I announced to her during a session that I was going to read the dream to her:

I am sitting in the passenger seat in a station wagon being driven by Mason, my youngest son. There is a frail looking minister-type man in a cheap polyester suit occupying the rear seat, and he and I are having a conversation. I inform him that I know what his next question will be. He says he doesn't believe I know what it will be. I confidently respond by saying that he is going to ask me whether or not I think change is possible. He is surprised that I guessed correctly, and I comment that I thought it was the only obvious question. Then he asks me if I think change is possible. I answer, "Yes, I know change is possible because of my analysis." I start to explain what I mean and while doing so, look to the left and see a train coming down the tracks. It almost hits us. We are surprised but keep moving, saying to each other, "We almost got hit."

When I stopped broadcasting my dream into my cell phone to reach the analyst, a dream that I hoped was chock full of transformational symbols, maybe a totem or two, I encountered a long pause, a gap that left me with the feeling that I was enduring an overly long concert intermission—I wanted the show to go on! Unable to wait any longer for feedback on my dream because even as I read it, I was losing interest. I just don't do dreams very well, I thought. So I decided to change the subject and interrupted the uncomfortable silence. This had been a silence riddled with anxiety that I wanted and didn't want to share with the analyst. Another uncomfortable subject came to mind, perhaps because I was traveling in the dream, this connected with a free association that snuck into my consciousness so confidently that I instantly blurted out what sounded like an accusation that I remembered she was going to be gone the next week. In reality, she was going to be absent from the office for two weeks.

Right about then the phone line went dead. We were disconnected. This had never happened before. Testing out my new maturity, I made a self-assessment and noticed what I felt once she was no longer on the line. To my amazement, what was present was a sense of relief, almost ease. Acting as my own therapist for a second or two, I decided the feeling of ease meant I would thrive during her upcoming absence and more astonishingly, that I would flourish after termination. This rumination took but a nanosecond and brought a smile to my face, a smile she would have surely analyzed if she could have seen me.

I then put my thumb on the little green icon on my cell phone and the next encounter took me by surprise: the process of reestablishing the connection took longer than expected given her usual stick-to-business demeanor. We discussed the disruption, both of us agreeing we didn't know any probable cause. For a few golden moments, it was as if we were chatting. That rarely happened, and I was enjoying it— my dream of being colleagues becoming temporarily true but then, without explanation, she returned to her professional tone and crisply articulated this surprising interpretation: "You need to slow down. Take the meat of the dream to see what you can learn." Why was she telling me to slow down? Did she hear me say that I knew she was going to be gone? I pulled the pillow down around my neck in an attempt to get comfy and slough off my irritation with her insinuation that I was once again rushing, being careful not to disturb the microphone which would make scratchy sounds she vehemently detested. Though in fact irritated, I unconsciously had reverted to my old habit of trying to keep her happy. I remained still as a corpse. I squinted my eyes as this transpired, looking as if I was about to ask a question. Then, apparently to entertain myself, I mouthed dramatically for my own amusement—meat?

The pause unfolded. It eventually occurred to me that by meat she was referring to the main characters in the dream. I made an executive decision to begin an exploration of the dream by dealing with the minister-type man who was sitting in the rear seat. Still grasping the cell phone with my earbuds buried firmly in place, I recalled how my mother befriended ministers in our local United Methodist church. Mom had great sympathy for the difficulties ministers faced in their vocation as pastors and lamented to anyone who would listen how underpaid they were. Mom was outspoken; she knew what was behind the scenes and could be a good listener. The combination of letting others know what she thought and being able to listen meant small-town pastors confided in her even though technically they were instructed not to be personal friends or have one-on-one relationships with people in their congregations. Mom didn't tell me everything these ministers confided in her, but it was enough that I, too, felt sympathy for the minister's predicament. This was the type of beleaguered fragile minister-man that I imagined had populated my dream. Someone trying to be helpful but with great needs of their own. Our session ended, as most did, with none of my questions solved but with a sense of satisfaction that I had gone deeply into my psyche.

After disconnecting from the call, in the resulting silence of my own making, I recalled that Freud was famous for his opus, *The Interpretation of Dreams* (Freud, 1955, 2010). It is a huge book—thick as the Bible. Drifting into a daydream-like state, I opened my copy that was providentially lying on my bedside table to see an unusual notation I'd made in black ink on the upper right-hand corner of Chapter 1. I had written, 7:40 PM, 10-1-2016. I remembered writing this because reading Freud's groundbreaking ideas on dreams had pushed me out of my normal way of thinking. I remembered that I didn't want to forget when I experienced this feeling of going beyond my normal reality. Had I felt the book sacred? I reread the first sentence of Freud's tome and felt once again why I was so moved by his words: "In the pages that follow I shall bring forward proof that there is a psychological technique which makes it possible to interpret dreams, and that, if that procedure is employed, every dream reveals itself as a psychical structure which has a meaning and which can be inserted at an assignable point in the mental activities of waking life."

After rereading this, I was aware of more reasons I wanted to be more skillful deciphering and learning from my dreams. Now I wanted to know more about my psychical structure. Maybe my dreams could assist me in working with the inner shaman. Or was I mixing metaphors? I knew that to decipher information from my dreams, I would have to practice interpreting them. As this eighth month of termination continued, I attempted to pay more than my usual lackadaisical attention to dreams and work with them to see what I could decipher. I felt clumsy trying to put words to the dream symbols. I wanted to feel sophisticated and knowledgeable, but I rarely did.

Occasionally in years past, when the analyst and I were physically in the same room, I shared dreams during a session, mostly dreams that had been scribbled down on scraps of paper when I woke up in the middle of the night. In the past when I'd commuted to the analyst's consultation room, I would cross her threshold clutching either these scraps of paper or I would carefully shelter my dream notebook in my arms with accompanying strict orders to myself not to forget it as I once did. I was curious if the analyst had peeked inside my left behind notebook at the dreams I had chosen not to present. I didn't ask her as I figured she wouldn't admit if she had snooped and simply asking the question would imply I didn't trust her.

Despite my new desire to work with dreams, I remained ambivalent about the significance of dreams, not feeling very competent at deciphering their meaning. I also wondered how valid interpretations could be when there were so many possible interpretations. I was learning that imagination was part of the unconscious and working to update my definition of imagination to include its helpful aspects. My perfectionism blocked me from wanting to work with my dreams. I had not realized fully how many ways each dream could provide assistance to the dreamer. The same dream could help in different ways. And that paying attention to the images and feelings was important in knowing oneself.

In every session of my lengthy psychoanalytic experience, especially in the final year of termination, I was encouraged to express myself in ways that had previously been discouraged. My parents and their parents and several generations before them, I would wager, kept stiff upper lips regarding life's travails. My analyst's modus operandi was in many ways the polar opposite of what felt natural to me and my heritage. Divulging deepest fears, verbalizing innermost secrets out loud that revealed literal and figurative dreams was clearly the psychoanalyst's agenda. Her consistent plea to disclose what I felt was unrelenting!

Initially, the analyst's plan had bothered me. When I began the process of classical Freudian psychoanalysis, I regarded myself as a sophisticated person who refrained from acting emotionally or out of control, a person who kept clear boundaries between reality and fantasy. I wanted to be intellectual, not silly spiritual. I didn't care about discussing feelings. I didn't value them. I wasn't aware that soon I would discover a wise inner shaman when I explored and began to weave together the secular and sacred and how working with my dreams would play a small part.

Perhaps becoming more aware of the spiritual realm and becoming more expressive in my conversations with the analyst was the result of the analytical couch continuing to be my own bed. Maybe it was the use of a virtual device that I was in the habit of speaking on with others as a way of blunting the isolation I was feeling because of the pandemic. I suppose it could have been that because analysis was coming to an end, I felt pressure to get it all out while I still had a chance. Whatever the cause, I began to notice an increasing level of freedom in my own speech.

I was drawn to the idea that every person had an inner shaman, sometimes known as the inner shamanic teacher. I learned that experienced shamans travelled to Otherworldly realms as they drummed for themselves or listened to drumming that had a regular trance-like beat. I loved the feeling of synchrony I felt when joining others in a rhythm, a rhythm that might be called collective effervescence. This vibrancy was what I remembered about my favorite activity during the New Zealand Shamanic workshop, which occurred when the group gathered in the darkness and unabashedly made noise. There were drums and rattles and voices. Sitting on the floor, I felt as if the creation of vibrations and harmonies, as they began to mingle and rise in intensity, was a very sacred event. We were all one and together for the crescendo that left us feeling lifted from the confines of the secular world. I wanted to share this with my sister Nina, so when she visited, I invited her to join me for an evening drumming circle. We connected deeply as sisters as we both loved to beat drums and join in what I like calling the effervescence. I remembered this evening fondly.

But now we were months into COVID-19, a pandemic with no foreseeable ending, so it felt as if going along with the analyst's plan to be more expressive, to really say what came up from my unconscious without censoring, was less risky. When it came to the fear of being infected by the virus, followed by the fear of loved ones being infected by the virus, shadowed by the fear of death for me and my loved ones from the virus or a variant, suddenly I expressed these fears and other subjects that I normally avoided.

I again remembered how my analyst had informed me she was going to be out of her office for two weeks in June. In the past, when she was out of the office, she handed me a sheet of paper with the dates she would be gone listed. In the past when she was gone for two weeks, they were consecutive weeks, so I assumed that would be the case as I diligently marked what I heard her say on my calendar. I did not notice that this year she was going to be gone one week, back a week, and then gone another week. I cannot imagine how I missed this; evidently, I was not paying attention. The analyst placed a call to me on Tuesday, June 23, 2020, to ask where I was. I was gobsmacked, as my friends in New Zealand would say. She informed me that she was in the office; she would be gone the next week. I was incredulous—I wouldn't make a mistake like that! That meant that I had missed my session with her on Monday for which I knew I would be charged.

I informed her, I'm sure with considerable irritation in my voice, that I would go get the piece of paper that she had given me with her out of the office dates and prove to her that she had informed me incorrectly. The only problem was that since I hadn't seen her in person for several months, there was not an actual paper with dates on it. She had given the dates to me on the phone; I had written them down myself. But I would have sworn I had a paper from her to prove she was wrong. When I realized my double mistake—the dates and the mistaken idea of a paper memo—I was humbled. Realizing how stubborn I could be and how much I wanted to blame others for my mistakes gave me a new sense of how I operated under stress. It was a valuable lesson in how much omnipotence I still operated with. All this happened internally, though I had the sense that she knew I knew. It was hard for me to apologize to her as my sense of omnipotence blocked the way.

When this awkward unexpected session was over, I felt stirred up. The analyst and I had coined the phrase 'above it all' to describe the type of behavior I had just exhibited. I found a synonym for omnipotent in my synonym finder that made me grin— it was: 'on high.' That's how I had felt in the past—feelings were something to be guarded against and risen above. Feelings could get you in trouble. I discovered in my reading that realizing one's omnipotence was an important first step. I was now paying attention to my behavior and letting go of the posture that cut me off from feelings and true intimacy with other people.

I was beginning to think about my inner shaman and the spiritual nature of Buddhism. So much was happening. With the termination period grinding to an end, the insistent drumbeat of wanting to know was easing, but it wasn't completely erased. I felt excitement about the future.

9

THE SPIRIT WORLD

July 2020

While I muttered curses toward a flat headed nail that continually slipped into the wall before I could flip and anchor the Natural Heritage calendar page from June to July 2020, I remembered walking on the pacific beach in San Diego with my middle son on his Independence Day birthday. This year, visiting him for his fifty-first birthday would not be happening. The *Des Moines Register*, read daily by my husband and me in the old-fashioned paper version, continued to report an increasing number of people being infected by COVID-19. Since we are in our seventies, we are in the high-risk group for the virus.

I found it hard to believe that next year Mark would be the age I was when my mother died. While I mused on this jarring juxtaposition of dates, it occurred to me that when mom was seventy-five, she died, and I would be seventy-five in three months. All these factors, plus my terror of this infectious disease ravaging the world, prompted me to feel my mortality in an immediate way.

As I contemplated death, I remembered reading how Michael Eigen, a noted psychoanalyst, recommended each person develop a relationship with what he referred to as "this unknowable thing" (Eigen, Faith and Transformation, 2011). I was pretty certain he was referring to having a relationship with death. I wondered if the unknowable thing I needed to relate to might be the idea that the time had come for me to combine the Spirit World, what I would say was my spiritual sense, with my new awareness of the secular world that had been developed during the years of analysis, or what I thought of as Freud's reality.

I reminded myself that this was, after all, the termination year of my over a decade of analysis. Soon this part of my secular life would cease. What would remain? For the present time, analytical sessions continued via cell phone, and I had to admit, the convenience of this arrangement was addictive. Sometimes I closed my eyes and pictured the analyst's calm, peaceful office. Included in the visualization was the analytical couch I had inhabited for so many years which in my dream-like state, resided in a perfect world. Coming out of my reverie, I opened my eyes to think realistically about her office, how often I froze the minute I crossed the threshold and how irritating and ineffective her synthetic blanket had been when I was shivering, especially in the summer when the arctic air conditioning kicked in. I was proud of myself for being able to see the whole picture. I hadn't always been able to do that.

July 2020 nudged us over the halfway mark of the year. Despite the less-than-ideal circumstances I was experiencing, I perceived in myself a sense of lessened anxiety. I was sleeping more soundly, having fewer digestive issues, and overall worried less about things I could not control. I felt connected to my family and friends even though I couldn't meet with them in person. I discerned that I was moving closer each month to taking a psychoanalytic worldview. When I stopped to think about this, I speculated this improvement was related to my encounters with otherness. It is a psychoanalytic paradox that in order for there to be intimacy, there has to be separateness or a sense of the other.

I knew that as an infant I had not automatically known otherness. It is common psychological knowledge that infants do not spontaneously acquire a sense of separateness when the umbilical cord is severed. I would wager that my initial sense of otherness began when the discomfort of my hunger was eased by the breast, though of course I have no memory of when that happened. The feeling of being a separate self also evolved when I was bathed in the loving gaze of my primary parent in addition to my paternal and maternal grandparents. This attention began the day I was born, October 10, 1945. My father as an "other" would not be physically available until December 15, 1945, when he returned to the family farm after proudly serving his country during World War II as a member of the U.S. Navy.

The feeling of being a separate organism, knowing an 'other,' comes as the result of mastering developmental tasks at each age group (infant to 18 months, 18 months to 3 years, 4–5, 6–11, and 12–18). Experts write that the tasks of each stage do not need to be fully mastered at each stage. I entered Freudian psychoanalysis in the decade of my sixties. I did not know how to react to otherness with acceptance and non-judgement.

Sigmund Freud's psychoanalytic theory promoted recognition of otherness because he realized, from his very early personal experience, how enticing it was to remain melded to an 'other.' Freud believed that human beings desired a return to the feeling of oneness, a state he once famously described as an oceanic feeling. This oceanic feeling replicated people's earlier experiences of oneness that he suspected occurred during an infant's first encounters with life. If one remained in infancy, also known as the togetherness stage, any discomfort encountered would have to be alleviated by someone else. If one did not consider the lack of freedom this would entail, this state seemed a paradise—until the ties that bind start to bind. The unconscious wish for merging, one that most humans experience, was what my analyst advocated that I was missing from my mother when siblings joined the household. This unconscious wish, as an adult, morphed into a desire to merge with a lover.

One of Freud's admired and respected friends, Romain Rolland, wanted Freud to believe that the energy behind the feelings Freud labeled oceanic were the true source of religion. Rolland tried to convince Freud this type of feeling was separate from the intellect and was connected with spirit. In contrast, Freud linked oceanic feelings to the primal ego feeling of the infant prior to the differentiation that took place between mother and child. Freud informed Rolland that he had never experienced this type of mystical feeling, that he was putting a label on experiences others had reported having. Freud believed that religious feelings were an adult phenomenon. He believed that the sensations people felt of oneness were not sourced by religious experience. Freud instead posited these feelings were the products of religious activity (Hewitt, 2014). In other words, there was not an outside source or supreme being producing the religious feelings—the feelings were generated by religious activities and ritual.

Initially, I thought my life experience more consistent with Rolland's than with Freud's ideas of promoting the rational. As I was reading about their differences, I cheered Rolland on, hoping he could convince Freud that the world contained a degree of magic. I remembered my own feeling of overwhelming oneness that occurred on one occasion that I had difficulty describing; it had felt different from anything else I remembered feeling, more like it was produced outside of me than inside. There had been no felt sense that it originated in my intellect. This memorable incident happened when I stepped out of the car at a lookout point after a long drive in the mountains. My body was overcome with feelings I was unable to describe, and my eyes saw sights previously unseen though I could not ascribe words to what I had witnessed. This was over thirty years ago, and I remembered it quite well. For many years, I believed the ultimate way of partaking in this otherworldly feeling was to experience it in a romantic relationship with a soul mate. By the time I was ready to terminate my analytical treatment, however, I was questioning that idea. Equals don't merge into one another. They live side by side.

I continued to read psychanalytic literature to increase my understanding of Freud's relationship with religion and the oceanic feeling. The most thorough investigation I found was in *Freud: An Intellectual Biography* by philosopher and psychoanalyst Joel Whitebook. Whitebook proposed that Freud's early disappointment in his mother led to his over-focus on independence and rejection of consolation.

One of the words I sometimes cautiously but unconsciously threw out in analytic sessions to impress the analyst was intersubjectivity. I loved the word for reasons I found difficult to explain. I think I must have run across it early in my psychoanalytic reading. Each time I uttered the word intersubjectivity, the analyst would ask me what I thought it meant. I would be garbled when trying to explain because I basically had no clear idea of what it meant, I just liked saying it. Discovering in the literature that the person most quoted on intersubjectivity was Jessica Benjamin, I purchased one of her books. Soon I could understand why the analyst asked me what the word meant—it is a complicated word, so maybe she also wanted to know!

Benjamin writes she began her research in the 1970s looking at mother-infant research. When the infant became able to recognize the mother, Benjamin felt it might be the beginning scaffolding for the idea of intersubjectivity (Benjamin, 2018). I wanted to understand more, so I kept reading. Benjamin found that infant development takes place in the context of interacting with a more developed person. This, I think, describes the idea behind the psychoanalytic relationship. The analyst has a more developed mind that the analysand can learn from. I will have to spend more time reading Benjamin's book to learn more why I resonate with the word intersubjectivity and what more it means about otherness.

As I continued the termination process, I kept discovering from my interactions with the analyst the importance of and the need I had for agreement with others. I realized this had been true for most of my life. Agreement, I discovered when I contemplated it, had the flavor of oneness, the type of feeling that Freud thought related to humans' earliest interactions in the world. It was painful and difficult, but I had to learn to recognize when I was manipulating others as a ploy to feel agreement, which if I then received would give me the oceanic feelings I craved. The analyst continued to use every interaction we engaged in to help me learn about myself and my dysfunctional patterns. For example, when I would phone her at our regularly scheduled time, she would answer by saying hello, to which I would reply, "This is Nicky." I continued doing this despite the fact that there was usually a feeling of awkwardness as she didn't respond to this introduction on my part. Dead silence was what I heard.

Eventually, the analyst and I talked about this uncomfortable interaction that kept happening. It was hard for me to hear but eventually I understood her point that when I said, "This is Nicky," I was wanting her to agree or respond in some positive way to what I had said. If she would have done this, it would have felt like approval to me, and I would have felt comfortable. Her point was that it wasn't her job to make me comfortable. There was not an actual reason I needed to say my name; she knew it was me as it was our scheduled time. She saw it as me trying to control her behavior.

In a similar situation, when I am dealing with an 'other,' I may try to convince this other person to tell me exactly what they want; then when I do it for them, it is to care for them, and I feel good because I knew what they wanted and provided it for them. Her point would be that this puts me in charge. When I can forego getting approval or feeling comfortable, I can move closer to authentic self-definition and individuation. It seemed paradoxical that the process of becoming separate happened in the context of a close relationship with an analyst. Often I felt an odd combination of uncertainty and pleasure; uncertainty as I reluctantly opened to her despite her interpretations that often felt hurtful, and pleasure that I was learning to relate in healthy ways.

Psychoanalysis was teaching me how to live in a more mature manner. I needed all the input I could find to keep growing. I was hungry for more input so on May 31, 2020, I listened to Warren S. Poland, a psychoanalyst for over fifty years, being interviewed on IPA Off the Couch podcast. I was moved by Poland's kindness and wisdom. The host, Harvey Schwartz, remarked that Poland's book, *Intimacy and Separateness in Psychoanalysis,* was a must read so I ordered it. When it arrived in July, I began underlining gems immediately. Here are words from Poland's text that encapsulate beautifully what I was trying to explain earlier: "For me, grasping reality always requires a stretch to try to realize what self and otherness mean, to struggle to contain with great difficulty the awareness that, while you and I share the same world, we have different and equally valid realities" (Poland, 1996).

Poland's book is one I will continue to read and study when

the termination process is complete. It is a much easier read for me than Benjamin's. One of the last times I perused it, I outlined the following words in a box: "What have we left out?" This seemed a profoundly psychoanalytic question. It seemed an appropriate question for me to ponder, especially when I revised it to "What have I left out?" This seemed especially true as I contemplated letting go of analysis. What have I left out?

When I answered this question, the first thing that came to mind was my spiritual nature. Essentially, I thought, I have ignored my spiritual nature. I've left it out of my analysis for fear of looking stupid. I stopped going to church. This omission took place once I started Freudian psychoanalysis in 2007. It wasn't very long after I started seeing the psychoanalyst that I drew a big black line between what I considered secular and what I felt was sacred. Before that, I took for granted that there were important spiritual aspects to my life. During analysis, I took seriously anything I deemed secular and for the most part, didn't place much importance on anything I thought too sacred. I thought it was too woo-woo. Now, as I entered the last few months of the termination process, I started to notice that the big black line wasn't so thick or definite anymore. What was secular and what was sacred?

I really began thinking about both of these questions, what have I left out and how do I define secular and sacred, on the day I read a Facebook (FB) post from Jim Newby. Jim, a Quaker minister, had been the leader of a spirituality discussion group I attended years ago. In our group we could talk about anything. I joyously followed him on FB, because I always felt very comfortable with his theology. The sentence in his post that resonated for me and helped me answer my questions was: "I believe, self-awareness and God awareness are one and the same." The self-awareness part spoke to me of the work I had done in analysis which I had deemed secular. The

God-awareness phrase caused minor distress because for many years, I felt uncomfortable with the word God. But I figured that since it was Jim using the word God, I could trust that he used it in an inclusive manner. It was becoming clear I would have to look into the definitions of secular and sacred.

These two questions followed me when I attended two half-day Zen retreats in July. Zen is a branch of Buddhism, and I knew that technically Buddhism is not a religion; rather, it is more of a philosophy. At one of the gatherings, the subject was the philosophical perspective on the meaning of liberation. There was talk of Daoism with Dao being the natural world. I wrote down that liberation is found by removing oneself from society, being alone. And that to be alone is to find true contentment. This contradicted the psychoanalytic idea that knowing how to interact with an 'other' is the ultimate way to find happiness. I would have to think about this.

The talk of removing self from other people renewed the lure of living a hermit-type life. This desire has been hidden deep inside me, fed by reading *Cave in the Snow: A Western Woman's Quest for Enlightenment* by Vicki Mackenzie and about Tenzin Palmo, a woman I met on one of my trips to India. When I was sitting on the floor next to Tenzin, I could scarcely believe that she was the woman I had read about who spent twelve years in a cave, all alone. She had huge hands that stood out in one of the pictures I took of her. I was thinking of her during the retreat. She had spent years meditating in a small box, the same box that she slept in. When the snow melted, everything she had with her got wet. Here I was, in a Zen retreat for three hours and inwardly complaining about feeling tired from having thirty-minute sitting periods. My back was hurting. It was difficult to keep my attention on the breath. How did she do it?

When I wasn't thinking about Tenzin, I heard the priest say that if you have an issue, be prepared to sit with it for ten years. I grinned to myself when I compared my time in psychoanalysis with what the Zen priest was recommending. I agreed when he mentioned that there is some benefit to not having an answer right away. The analyst would never answer a direct question. We were advised to not think in terms of good or bad or judge whether something is true or false. The Zen practice of zazen, which simply means sitting meditation, will provide us with an opportunity to get away from duality.

I kept hearing and seeing things I hadn't paid attention to before. Was self-awareness and God-awareness one and the same? In order to have sacred qualities, was it necessary to hibernate in a cave? What was the spirit world going to be for me?

10

ACCEPTANCE

August 2020

Suddenly August arrived. The word 'suddenly' appeared in my mind, never mind knowing that *nothing* happens suddenly. This was not the first time the word suddenly sneaked past the censors and creeped into my vocabulary. Despite my imperfect memory, I remembered times in the past when I had uttered: "Suddenly it's dark!" or "Suddenly I am starving." When these phrases came out of my mouth, despite knowing rationally that neither darkness nor hunger happens in a flash, I felt they contained a dollop of emotional truth.

Chogyam Trungpa wrote that everything takes time to develop. Trungpa, a controversial Buddhist priest many believe is responsible for bringing Buddhism to the West, wrote that even so-called instant enlightenment requires preparation. When people use the word suddenly, he wrote, it usually indicates an effort was being made to add drama or magic to the situation.

The year was 2020, and perhaps I used the word suddenly because I needed drama to accept this later stage of the termination process. I was closer to the end than the beginning. Maybe I wanted excitement in this month of August, the month two of my sisters ordinarily make a pilgrimage from Colorado to Iowa for the Iowa State Fair. Despite unprecedented cancellation of the fair this year, my siblings decided to make the trip, anyway. They planned to stop at our home for a quick visit and a masked walk on the nature trail. Because of psychoanalytic training by my analyst, I paid attention and noted that their impending visit aroused in me oldest sister characteristics of a negative—one might say pathological—nature. Stay home, my inner bossy voice shouted! My underlying fear: they will bring COVID-19 with them, exposing me and my husband to the deadly virus.

Personally, I would not take a trip anywhere with COVID-19 infections running rampant in our state and the entire country. Warnings not to touch counters in public restrooms or eat indoors in restaurants remind me to stay home. My sisters seem fearless to me, and I have not yet determined whether or not theirs is an admirable fearlessness. Maybe a foolish fearlessness? Or perhaps I am too fearful?

For many years I have been fascinated with Freud's ideas concerning psychosomatics, the way the mind influences the body. The pandemic has elicited increased thinking about the mind-body connection. Does my mind have a big influence on whether or not I get infected? I am disappointed that Freud didn't do more to explain the mind and body connection. I wonder how the body is affected by the spirit, let alone the more current issue of wondering how my body would handle this new virus. One of my sisters believes in the power of positive thinking and the law of attraction, both of which have a spiritual origin. If my sisters think only positive thoughts, will they be safe? Does the mind have that much control over the body? Or was this magical thinking?

My desire to feel more accepting of my long-held beliefs and integrate my new way of thinking has presented me with huge challenges. Historically, I have resonated with the sentiment that God is love. Now I am sensing the connections between all sentient beings. However, the secular sentiments of Freud's psychoanalytical theory with the focus on external reality have temporarily trumped my budding notions of what I deem sacred in my life. It suddenly (sic) occurs to me that not counting the rest of this month, I have only thirty-four analytical appointments remaining. I want to acknowledge I have realized that hearing the actual number of sessions remaining probably will not affect you in the same way as it does me. In the more usual type of therapy, for example, if you were attending therapy sessions with a cognitive psychologist once a week and you were told that you had thirty-four more sessions, you would be looking at approximately eight months remaining. In that kind of treatment, it may be doubtful you would need thirty-four more sessions. In today's world of brief therapy, the contract stipulated between therapist and client would be to fix one problem or issue and in practical terms, six sessions may be all the insurance covered.

The deep psychological change made possible by Freudian psychoanalytic treatment makes it difficult for me to have faith in short-term therapies. They offered Band-Aids that did not cure my underlying issues. The problem-solving short-term variety may not have worked for me because I didn't present one problem to work on when I was in brief therapy. I have always wanted to work on deeper issues that brief work wasn't cut out to handle. In actuality, I needed to feel the despair I had been avoiding and accept responsibility for my life in its totality. This did not happen for me in short-term therapy. I had to give up the idea that I was in charge of the transformation I requested. I was asking for a process of deep transformation that would require years. Even now, knowing as I do in this termination period how much my life has been enriched by this process, I still wonder at times what my life would have been like if I had bid farewell to the analyst after one year. Of course, there is no way of knowing.

In psychoanalysis I have learned to become more of a separate self. I have my own ideas that I work to clarify and express. The change happened so gradually in my mind that it is hard to describe what is actually different about me now. Since psychoanalysis is designed to be an ongoing process, some analysands find the process so valuable, they never end their sessions. Although I am terminating psychoanalysis, I would not say that I am completely finished as there is always more to learn about how the mind works.

I realize there will never be an ideal time to bid farewell to the analyst and the process but when I look at the days that will follow directly after my last session, I shudder. I want to sink into acceptance of the decision to terminate analysis, but it seems it will be very difficult as four days after my last session with the analyst, which of course will be held on the phone with my earbuds tucked deeply in my ears to keep her close, the United States of America will elect a new president. I desperately want a different president and I feel a great deal of excitement about the possibility of having a woman of color as vice president. My husband, who opines he does not approve of the current president one hundred percent, is pleased with how the current administration has boosted the economy. I know the economy is important, but I have never before rubbed shoulders with anyone who placed more importance on the job market than on the delivery of human services. My partner would say, at least I think he has said in the past, that I am comparing apples and oranges, that the two examples I gave are not related. Perhaps in his mind they aren't—but in my mind they are.

In analysis, which is coming rapidly to a close, I have received input on the project I am facing of how to be married to someone who, in some areas, is so different from what I am accustomed. The analyst has helped me stay mindful that no matter what I do or say, there is no way to change him. And also she reminded me frequently that my views are not the only correct ones. It is difficult to comprehend and then admit that the way I have experienced the world is only one way to approach things. The analyst not only has helped me broaden my views this way, but also helped me examine how the character traits of the current president, a person with characteristics that I can safely say I abhor, are parts of myself that I am not yet aware of. I hate knowing these similarities, but I can feel how true they are. It is very humbling and embarrassing to admit that when I angrily lash out at my husband, that when I feel judgmental, that when I am not articulate when I speak and use the same language over and over, I am just like him. I do not want to join the chorus of people who are nasty to the current administration as the people in government are not all bad, though without the analyst's help, I wonder if I will continue to hold this more neutral viewpoint.

I want to be married to my partner. He is a decent, honest, generous, and loving man. He makes me laugh. I love him and he loves me. I am learning about myself and the world by living with this person I respect but differ from. I am learning how to be in the world in a different way. In my former life as a social worker, I felt safe and comfortably at ease in the human service world. The people I related to all agreed that helping people needed to be the primary focus. We didn't focus much on the economy. The business world, which I have a closer relationship to because of my spouse, seems short sighted and less dangerous.

The psychoanalytic process with its analytic attitude, an attitude created and promoted by Sigmund Freud, has been influential in confronting my habitual need to see things as either black or white. Sometimes I observe a similar all-or-nothing attitude in the political arena. I want to understand and be more comfortable dealing with increased complexity so I can forgo taking sides. I don't want to politically be the type of red or blue person who demonizes the other side. A mature viewpoint would give me the ability to tolerate contradictions, which is an essential skill as many situations in the world are paradoxical. Having the ability to take a broader viewpoint has opened windows for me. I can see both sides of an issue. I don't get so reactive. I am able to feel more compassionate for all people. But I am wondering how I will hold on to my hard-earned changes and new ways of being in the world when I don't have the analyst to confront me and then support me.

As the month unfolded, I began to struggle for a mature way to feel regarding termination. A way to accept what will come in a couple of months. Buddhists, I've learned from my reading and hearing Dharma talks, accept what is in the present moment and at the same time, keep in mind how everything keeps changing. Buddhists call it impermanence. Perhaps, it occurred to me, it will help me terminate analysis if I understand Buddhist psychology. I was happy to discover that Chogyam Trungpa, the person I mentioned earlier this month who spoke to the idea that nothing happens suddenly, has written a book about the Buddhist approach to psychology, *The Sanity We Are Born With*. My initial reading of this book revealed Buddhist psychology had things in common with Freudian psychoanalysis. Of course, there were also differences. I decided to keep reading and making comparisons.

When a Zen priest in my area, Daishin, announced that one of his teachers, a woman from Japan, would be speaking for a two-hour workshop on Zoom, I paid my $15 quickly. I didn't want to miss it. Buddhism and Psychoanalysis are heavily populated with men, so hearing from a woman appealed to me. Yuko Yamada, my teacher's teacher, was in Japan when she spoke so the connection wasn't perfect on Zoom. It was clear enough that I could see and hear her. She looked very old and lively but when she started to speak, I felt myself settling back in my chair accompanied by a feeling of disappointment. I began to wonder if this was going to be worth my time. It was difficult to understand her, and the screen kept freezing. I was restless.

Despite acceptance of my newfound knowing that suddenly is not a real possibility, my mind jumped suddenly back in time, depositing me in a daydream of 1994. My friends Jo and John were leading a tour to India that I had signed up for. My reverie pictured us visiting a suburb of Dharamshala high in the Himalayas where the Dalai Lama lived in exile. Most fortunately, John's request for a private audience had been granted. My daydream reminded me I was not yet fifty years old, had been married to my first husband for thirty years.

My daydream reminded me, as it touched into the bruised place in my heart, that this was the husband who would betray me multiple times, lying convincingly to my credulous self. The husband who was employed as a lay administrator for a large protestant church, which undoubtedly gave him credibility in my unconscious mind. His powerful position meant we were surrounded by committed Christians. In this trance-like-state I was suddenly in, I recalled how thoroughly I had learned the minutiae of the Christian church hierarchy and Christian devotional literature.

This daydream vision then morphed to meditating with a Zen group in town and attending zazen sittings in their Zendo, which was located in a deteriorating mansion. I met with them before going across town to a Sunday School class that I attended with my family. The silence experienced in the Zendo left me relaxed and contemplative, but I found it difficult to either maintain or let go of the contemplative stance in order to join the social conversation required in Sunday School class. In the daydream, I reminisced about my peers in class who mistakenly thought of me as a pastor's wife, and who were totally surprised when I confided that I craved to sit in Zazen with Buddhists. These memories evoked a joke that I had loved to tell anyone who would listen, though neither group found it as humorous as I did. People in the Zen group had used a word that sounded to me like chicken tacos. They were really saying the word shikantaza, I found out much later, a word which had nothing to do with food but meant sitting in meditation precisely.

Reluctant to give up my fantasizing, I began remembering the books I had devoured by Christian authors. How I had tucked Henri Nouwen's Latin American Journal in my backpack to India; savored Madeleine L' Engle when she shared in her journals the difficult parts of family·life including problems in her marriage; learned from Martin Israel, much to my dismay, that suffering was indeed included in spiritual growth. It felt good to remember these books that were so important to me and now shelved carefully in the lower level of my home.

My daydream began to wind down as I flashed back to India and being seated on a cushion across the small lavishly decorated room from the spiritual leader of Tibetan Buddhism, His Holiness the Dalai Lama. I was disarmingly unaware of the honor and privilege I had been granted. I proceeded to judge him as silly and not very interesting in his childlike demeanor. I did not know that his grasp of the absolute, a word I would later learn from my Zen friends, meant that he could tune into the dimension of reality in which each and every thing is part of a seamless whole. He could see the oneness of everything, and it made him happy, but I didn't yet, and I remembered that I was not feeling as happy as he appeared.

So banishing these thoughts, though envisioning them had been entertaining, I continued to lean back in my chair as I contemplated this pensive daydream. I wondered what message I was to be receiving from this woman in Japan, Yuko Yamada. I started to pay attention. I sat up straighter. I remembered early on in the talk hearing her announce that she was going to present three subjects, but the only one I could recall was connection. But the three subjects—I grinned to myself about how much Buddhists liked numbered lists—turned out to be the least important of what I received from her. What did I get from Yuko Yamada? My journal noted that the idea of being simple and silly and real was what being in the present moment is all about. Yuko, like the Dalai Lama, had obviously processed her emotions. I liked her. Since I knew that my reverie had interfered with my listening, I wondered how I could learn more about her now that the Zoom meeting was over.

I emailed Daishin to inquire if he had suggestions for how to learn more about her. He referred me to a *Tricycle* article that proved to be a fascinating read. The main theme of her article was about the difficulty she encountered when she was asked to give up what her ego wanted. When I realized this was her struggle and that her struggle was similar to my struggle, I was very moved. Can I feel acceptance towards my struggles, I wondered?

II

Vision

September 2020

Sixty-five years ago on September 2, 1955, a month before I would turn ten on the tenth of October, my mom gave birth to a third sibling, my second sister, Nan. Many years when I turned the calendar page to view the month of September, I chastised myself for forgetting to send Nan's birthday card so it would arrive on her special day. This year, my self-chastisement was not about forgetting to send Nan's card. I had remembered. As the oldest daughter of five, I religiously tried to follow the family rule that dictated we send at least one physical greeting card in honor of each person's birthday. The inner turmoil when greeting September this year was of a different sort. This angst concerned the dearth of time remaining in my psychoanalytic treatment. After all, September was the next to last month of life-giving analytic sessions conducted by a skilled psychoanalyst. It's time to wake up, I admonished myself. Time to be certain I had analyzed everything that needed to be analyzed.

One unconscious troublesome character trait I had confronted in analytic sessions and dealt with in my personal life was my need to know. If you asked me, "Know what?" I would say—know everything I need to know. I was convinced that if I just knew whatever I thought I didn't know, I would be able to solve conflicts, lessen anxiety, and fix whatever needed fixing. This knowing, if I could figure out how to attain it, would grant me assurance that the whole shebang, in other words whatever I faced, would turn out perfectly.

I owe a great deal of my clarity regarding this embedded in the family characteristic, one that I of course had unconsciously adopted, to Reverend Robert Crum. Bob was the director of a multi-ministry center that he felt was a refuge for anyone who needed care. He met my mother at my oldest son's high school graduation open house and pulled me aside afterwards to share this observation: "Your mother really wants to know!" The meaning of his remark wasn't instantly apparent to me, but his words were soldered in my mind for eternity. It took me years to untangle the information he had distilled and shared from one conversation with my mother. After several years of pithy psychoanalytic interpretations offered by the analyst, one-liners that fit the situation perfectly but stopped me in my tracks, it occurred to me that Bob had been tuned into one way my mother could be off-putting, but he used non-judgmental language to describe it to me. It took additional effort, time, and analyst input to admit to myself that I, too, wanted to know as a way to shore my sense of well-being.

Mom's need to know came out as questions, questions designed by her unconscious desire to be the perfect mother. The queries seemed to me designed for the purpose of making sure she would never do anything wrong or upset anyone. When she came to visit me after my first child was born, I about went crazy answering all her questions even though I knew she was trying to please me. Her questions were not philosophical or existential questions that would bring us closer in our understanding of each other. The constant barrage of inquiries about where this dish went or how this towel was to be folded nearly drove me crazy. I remember feeling shame at my fury. After all, she was being generous to come and help me adjust to my new role as a mother.

During one of my September analytical sessions, the analyst snuck the word omnipotence in to describe behavior. Was she talking about my mother? She's used the word before, but I pretty much ignored it. The word sounded too pathological for my taste. This, of course, speaks to how I resisted transformation, and as Freud would have said, analysands in analysis resist every step of the way. Much to my surprise, this resistance continued to operate even in the last few months of treatment. Freud's point was that for every advance to a higher stage of psychical organization, the analysand, in this case me, creates a new form of censorship. In this case, I continued to block out, censor, and ignore the word omnipotent. Needing to know the unknowable was what both Mom and I wanted. We both liked to be in control. Our belief that knowing would lessen suffering was a mistaken notion. The analyst undoubtedly described our efforts to control as omnipotent behaviors. Part of waking up was finding my humility and that would come gradually. I can now admit that I don't know.

Occasionally throughout the years of analysis, I would bring up a movie or Netflix series to use as an example of behavior I wanted to explore without getting too personal. In one particular September session, I mentioned two characters from the very intense *Outlander* series we were watching, both of whom could be considered omnipotent. They were both in control and felt they could shape reality to their liking. There was nothing they couldn't do. Since fear was a topic that popped up repeatedly during my treatment, I wanted to share with the analyst how I admired Claire Fraser (played by Caitriona Balfe), who was the main time-traveling female star. Claire was so courageous, and I wanted the analyst to know that despite my fears, I recognized courage when I saw it. I was worried she thought I was a wimp since I shared all my fears with her. I wanted her respect.

The episode I reported on was when Claire had jumped off a ship with only the help of a woman who didn't speak her language. I was becoming aware that not many people spoke the language of psychoanalysis, so I related strongly to this leap into the vastness of the ocean. My fear of water and getting lost, both of which had been discussed with the analyst many times in great detail, meant that Claire's leap into the ocean was extremely hard for me to watch. Especially so because she didn't know what country she would end up swimming to or what direction she would be headed. I marveled at her ability to jump out of the ship without knowing any of this. After this session, I wrote in my journal that I hated to write about what happened in the session where I had shared Claire's bravery as it was too complicated and difficult to describe. Mostly I think that I feared it wasn't very sophisticated material. I wanted to abandon the journal, pick a fight with someone, find someone to blame for the difficulty I was feeling at the time. But using Claire as a role model, I kept writing even though I didn't know for sure where it would lead me. But as I write this, I see a metaphor that is powerful and sophisticated. How about this: I leapt into the ocean of society where people, for the most part, don't speak my preferred language of psychoanalysis.

The other character I talked about with the analyst was Jamie Fraser, Claire's husband (played by Sam Heugham). If there was trouble to be found, Jamie found it. His omnipotence got him out of many close calls but almost backfired in the episode I described to the analyst. Jamie had been locked up by the bad guy, Jonathan Randall (played by Tobias Menzies), a villain so distasteful that I had a physical reaction to his evil ways. When he came on the screen, I would clench my fists and sometimes close my eyes or moan "oh no, oh no" when he was doing something particularly vile. In this episode, Jamie tried to enlist a young unskilled boy, a person he knew from his small town, to help get him out of the prison where he was being held. Jamie was so driven to escape that he wasn't thinking clearly and trusted the boy whom anyone could see would never be successful. I discussed with the analyst how obvious it was that Jamie was making a bad decision and that I identified with his driven-ness. I thought that the analyst believed that driven-ness and omnipotence had similar characteristics.

After I explained my connection to Jamie and why I brought him to the session, the analyst said, "It sounds like you feel the boy and me were pushing against you." I wondered what on earth she meant by this interpretation. It felt like it came out of the blue, but it also felt somehow right though I couldn't explain it, even to myself. Maybe she was insinuating that when caught in the throes of driven-ness, I made bad decisions? A part of me realized that I was being encouraged to give up my lifelong omnipotent stance. After this full, rich, and confusing session, I did something I had never done before. I sent the analyst a text. It said, "Thank you for helping me face my omnipotence. A fierce battle indeed." I was astonished at her return text: "That is the fight that we took on." While in the past I had wanted her to praise me, admire me, treat me like a colleague, when I saw these words, they felt better than anything I had wanted. The words cemented our connection in my opinion. And then my next thought was, how will it ever be possible to give up this relationship?

Labor Day, September 7, 2020, the analyst wasn't in the

office, so I had the entire day for myself. My husband wanted to read and work on his jigsaw puzzle. I was eager to see Christine Valters Paintner on a live feed from Ireland as part of the twelve-week class I had enrolled in. This new live online class for 2020 was sponsored by the Abbey of the Arts, Paintner's online monastery. I love the tagline for the group: "Contemplative Living Through Contemplative and Expressive Arts." I had high hopes for this twelve-week seminar, as it had been eight years since I had taken a workshop with Christine. The termination phase of my psychoanalysis seemed to be unleashing my longing to dip back into my spiritual side. The timing of the class felt perfect as it would not end until late in November, long after I had said goodbye to my analyst. I figured it would help me with the transition.

Christine promised to expound on the characteristics of the inner monk and the artist, both described as energetic archetypes or patterns. I wondered how different her ideas would be from 2012 when I participated in a class based on the book *The Artist's Rule*, a book that she had signed and mailed to me. I was tickled to see the dedication that she made directly to me, Nicky, even spelling my name correctly. She had written: "May the journey ahead nourish your inner monk and artist. Warmest blessings." I read the first chapter of *The Artist's Rule* and skimmed others as the 2012 online class continued, but I didn't put into practice the spiritual practices she offered. After all, I was a Freudian analysand. It was important to me to separate the secular and the spiritual in order to be loyal to Freud and keep my own sense of sophistication. I didn't want to be fooled, so while I participated in the class, I didn't integrate her words into my life during that time period.

I had never met Christine in person, but I felt a connection to her. She had responded briefly several times after I had expressed appreciation for her words and work. Christine shared her chronic health issues, diseases that limited her stamina. I wanted to see her in person through the live videos to see how she was really doing. I had been impressed with her move from California to Ireland with her husband. She had written conversational yet literate books that I wished I had written. She was the type of Christian who appreciated the feminine, our ancestors, and art. I had followed Christine online for several years though I had never experienced her live online. This was the primary reason I enrolled—that and the chance to be in breakout rooms with other participants. I wanted to meet others who spoke my language. My marketing part wondered if they might be possible customers for my memoir when it would be available next month.

Christine's live video talks encouraged us to pay attention and be totally present for holy moments. She described synchronicities as a blessing of awareness—a definition that I appreciated because I experienced what my husband termed coincidences frequently. They held greater meaning to me than mere coincidence, but I hadn't known how to get to the level of meaning I felt. No sooner would I think of calling someone and the phone would ring. They had been thinking of me.

Paintner described the inner monk as one who has characteristics of slowness, spaciousness, being present to the mystery of living in the world; this description hadn't changed from 2012, I noted. I loved this definition and wanted to live more in that style. The artist was described as a person longing for creative expression, searching for joy and purpose which could be for one's own self or others. The artist connects to grief in a way that is larger than the ordinary feeling people have when they lose things that are important to them. These ideas were not new to me either, but I felt nourished by hearing them again. I wanted my life after analysis to have all these characteristics.

Christine described both the monk and the artist as edge dwellers and commented that living on the edge can be thrilling as well as terrifying. I didn't remember this part from the last class. It felt important to me. I compared these characteristics to the results of my time in psychoanalysis, and it resonated with me, especially when she said that love is the center of living on the edge and love is expressed through beauty. I remembered how Freud had written that psychoanalysis was a cure by love. I felt some connections beginning to happen.

The breakout groups consisted of women from many states and countries, but the sharing time was too short to make lasting connections. There were four sessions in September, and while I didn't feel that I was learning anything too new, the Christian underlying foundation felt familiar and comfortable, if at times, a bit too sweet and unsophisticated. I liked it when she spoke of walking as a way to be embodied. Christine used the word God occasionally, and I didn't have the negative reaction that I did in years past. I assumed that she was thinking of God as the pattern that connects because she used the word freely and didn't explain further.

In the past, when people had used the word God, I wanted them to tell me what they meant by the word. It didn't take long for my mind to create the childhood image of a male on his throne in the clouds when I heard the G word from most people. That didn't occur for me in this 2020 class. Christine referred frequently to Benedictine spirituality. St. Benedict's values, at least the ones she quoted like hospitality, community, and service, were inclusive and modern in scope.

Christine presents as a gentle soul with knowledge and courage that I wish I had. She spoke clearly without frogs in her throat. She was articulate. I envied her marriage to a man who shared her Christian beliefs as I was disappointed when my new husband's initial interest in my spiritualty didn't continue after we were married. I wondered if his non-spiritual views were influencing me. I hoped not. I hoped that my analysis had helped me develop a solid sense of self. Most days I thought it had.

Occasionally, I thought maybe I was more like my mother than I thought. Was my draw to spirituality related to the need to know—our need to know? I wondered about this the day after the initial art and monk class. The very next day was the seventh monthly class with Buddhist teacher Michael Carroll. The class had begun in March and was always on Mondays at 2:00 PM, which meant that I had to leave it a few minutes early to attend my analytical session on time.

When September's Monday class fell on a holiday, Labor Day, it was changed to Tuesday, at exactly the same time that my Tuesday analytical session was scheduled. Being with Carroll live (there were tapes I could listen to, but those had a different feel to me and there was no chance to ask questions) was important to me, so I asked the analyst if we could change our scheduled time and she agreed. I had never before asked her to change our time, so the decision itself informed me that the class was more important than I believed. I didn't tell the analyst why I wanted to change the time. She doesn't tell me her reason for changing the schedule. This interaction created a one-professional-to-another feeling.

But I wondered what it was about this class, the title of which was Buddhism in Modern Life, that kept me tuning in after six months' worth of classes. Carroll was a likable man with a sense of humor that bordered on rebelliousness toward dogma. I wanted to connect with him personally but had difficulty finding a working email address for him. I was aware that I wanted to be his special student, but I was also a bit intimidated by him. I didn't want to miss any insights he had about how Buddhism fit with modern life. In the initial class back in March, he hooked me with his initial announcement: Humans are endowed but something is off. I realize that out of context, this may not be understandable, but it made total sense to me. This proclamation reminded me of the difficulty I had specifying why it was that I entered psychoanalysis. I wasn't in a crisis. I wasn't in pain. Why did I ask for a referral for depth therapy?

The succinct answer Carroll provided to answer the question was nothing fancy or complicated. It was simply that something was off. I didn't articulate my reasons that way or conceptualize them using those words, but I knew exactly what he meant. It was accurate in a way that, while difficult to explain, provided legitimate reasons for my 2007 decision to enter analysis. Carroll explained to me and to the other class members that we were in the same position as Siddhartha—the man who became known as the Buddha. Siddhartha's life plan, orchestrated by an overly protective father unbeknownst to Siddhartha, was that Siddhartha would never encounter pain or suffering. This meant for all practical purposes, Siddhartha would be imprisoned in the family's castle. He would be safe and protected. But one day when he was allowed to run an errand with his servant, he witnessed an old beggar lying down on the street. He wanted to know more about what it was he saw. This was the beginning of his new life. A life where he would, instead of being protected, engage whole-heartedly in the dilemma of being human. For Siddhartha, this was the time period when his life was not going as planned; something was not working out as he expected. Carroll described this feeling as comparable to something tickling us.

But the fact is, according to Carroll, when things aren't going all that well, it can be good news. He advised us that both the states of uncertainty and of disappointment are more invitation than threat. Carroll proposed that an awareness of dysfunction means that something in us is waking up. I related to this. I remembered being upset when the analyst didn't succumb to my charms the way most everyone else did. It took me years to realize interpretations, especially the ones I rejected, misunderstood, or took offense at, were an invitation for me to be a real person, not the egotistic, above it all woman who didn't feel her feelings.

September was a short month. This year it felt shorter than usual. With each session being the last September session I would ever experience with this analyst in this unique type of relationship, I experienced feelings. Sorrow or relief. Analysis was a place where I faced reality and found myself. Towards the end of our last session in September, she said to me, "Ending analysis is killing me." Yes, I thought, I am killing you. She then added that "Ending analysis is making you dead." Taking these metaphorically, I can find the truth in them. I am killing the relationship we have. The part of me that needs to let go of the process feels deep grief. How can I let go? How can I hang on?

12

SECOND REALIZATION

October 2020

October 2020, the last month of my analysis. Psychoanalysts have employed the macabre word termination to describe the discontinuation of the unpredictable process of psychoanalytic treatment. While the word termination is fraught with images of finality and death, when I set aside my apprehensive feelings and attune to and trust the new alignment between the sacred and the secular, I am ready. Ending my involvement with Freud's particular method of discovery and change has required one calendar year. Termination, a descriptive word, was undoubtedly coined by a professional psychoanalyst who understood psychoanalysis. A person who knew the importance of giving the analysand (in this case me) a word serious enough to startle, to slow down, to make certain analysands knew what was at stake. Time to wrestle with the ambivalence caused by the internal struggles inevitably present when the decision to cease centering one's life around multiple psychoanalytic sessions each week is made. As this final month of formal classical psychoanalytic treatment continued to unfold, vague memories of when I had previously contemplated aborting the analytical process surfaced.

Severing the relationship with the analyst was an impulse that occurred several times during the years of treatment. Time in analysis did not feel linear. Non-linearity is present because the past lives in each of the present moments that make up the analytical hour. Walking into the analyst's consultation room four times a week (or during the eight months of pandemic, preparation to lie on my bed for a session), I agreed to participate in another way of being, of thinking, one that's hard to explain. It was known in psychoanalysis as free association and required a skill that was not natural for me. I noticed with satisfaction that my free associations had become easier to capture now in October than they had been in January. An example: during a number of October sessions lying on my bed, I remembered how I had tried to find patterns in the randomly dotted white suspended ceiling tiles that covered the ceiling in the analyst's office. Now, propped up on my bed, I noticed never before seen spikey patterns that resembled viral COVID-19 particles on the batik piece of art hanging on the opposite wall. As you can tell from this example, free association doesn't lead to normal conversation between intimates. Free association spirals down and digs up unresolved issues that one has repressed, in this case, my fear of COVID-19.

Over the years I grew more comfortable with long pauses that occurred while I was paused waiting for an association to surface in my mind, knowing that the analyst would not intervene no matter how long it took me or how many pleading prayers I silently offered for her intervention. The analyst appeared to have ample time to wait. The normal pressure to be efficient and accomplish goals didn't correspond with the psychoanalytic process we were engaged in. Thoughts did not follow the usual conscious threads that are expected in normal conversation.

Psychoanalysts believe that when a new utterance does not appear to have a link to the previous spoken word, the link that provided an obvious connecting point, it is an indication that the unconscious has been activated. There have been rumors that the unconscious is where the creative process abides. Analysts have been trained to believe the unconscious has a logic of its own and that the analyst's job is to connect the seemingly unconnected bits that the analysand offers while free-associating and in the process, discover how the analysand's mind works. My analyst recognized my secure and insecure states of mind as they fluctuated depending on numerous factors.

As the heart-shaped leaves on the redbud tree outside my bedroom window gently drifted to the ground, I experienced a dawning realization that the complex analytical interactions, exchanges I had come to depend on, were about to drop off from my life. I hoped that the absence of sessions would morph into presence as I wanted to prove the words, *absence is presence*, words I had written in my first memoir, were true. Flooded with feelings, the psychotherapist part of me deduced that these feelings spoke highly of my time with the analyst as she was the one who had helped me locate and express them.

During a session on October 13, I connected with what I deemed was a genuine free association: termination had things in common with dying. You knew it was going to happen. You couldn't change it. Part of me knew that if not ending analysis was my true desire, I could call off the termination process and continue in analysis and this, while it felt like an option I wouldn't take, felt powerful. I would be in charge. Halfway through the session, while pushing my earbuds deeper into my ears in order to hear her more clearly and connect with her more intimately, I heard myself spontaneously saying exactly what I was thinking: "I will miss you."

This may have been a subtle implication that our work was done, that I was ready to begin the grief process of leaving her, but that's not what she heard or had in mind—she still wanted me to work: "It occurs to me that you arrange it, so you don't have to end things." All I could manage to say was yes because I knew her words generally proved true. I thought of all the groups I had organized and how most of them went on for twenty years or more or until people moved away from our city. I responded to the analyst with a tinge of self-righteousness: "I ended it with my first husband." Her response: "After a long time of not ending." I wondered how would I continue to encounter my omnipotent unconscious without her help. I grinned to myself and murmured under my breath; I bet she will miss me too.

As October and the letting go continued, I struggled not to get overwhelmed by feelings. Who knew there could be so many? I remembered that in the not so distant past, I would have blocked out these feelings, climbed to the defended place I had labeled—we had labeled—being above it all. At times it was tempting to regress, ignore the feelings, go to the higher plane where I knew I could find temporary comfort and safety by ignoring my feelings. But I rejoice in not rising above it all, especially when I read that Freud idealized his early childhood and cut off from his feelings. This is difficult stuff, I think, when even the creator of psychoanalysis has difficulty facing unvarnished reality. Beginning to let go of my conviction that the relationship with the analyst was the only place I could find aliveness in my emotional landscape, I listened intently on October 14, 2020, when I attended a virtual Buddhist workshop. When I heard Buddhists speak of Right Action and Right Speech, I knew they too were yearning for the aliveness that came from the truth. Freud wasn't the only one who was searching for reality.

Buddhist psychology and Freudian psychoanalytic theory work towards helping people be comfortable in their own skins. Both speak of the discomfort of becoming conscious. Both teach how to sustain a paradoxical capacity to know and not know. As I listened to the various speakers, I realized that the capacity to engage with emotion or understand the aversion to doing so, what I had learned in psychoanalysis, was not only Freud's idea. Buddhists from the Shambala tradition that I was listening to said many of the same things that I had learned in my work with the analyst. Both systems are clear: when we open and stay in reality, we receive love, insight, real wisdom, and innovative clarity.

When I began exploring the world using increasingly secure bases, I realized that being alive was a privilege. The Open Heart Project was one of my secure bases. This was a place where I learned about Tibetan Buddhism, and in addition, how to respect the word imagination, developing an understanding of imagination as a direct personal perception that happens internally. I'm imagining that after the last session at the end of this month, I will continue to pay homage and attention to my psychic life while remembering that many of the problems I face, I made for myself. Problems become issues when I refuse to face reality. I am excited to perceive multiple ways the sacred and the secular overlap. On the sacred side, I will pursue an immanent orientation that sacralizes life—that finds the holy everywhere. Life without analysis will be a challenge. Life where I will give myself permission to honor all I have learned in analysis and all I have learned from Buddhism and all I have learned about Christian mysticism—the latter of which I haven't spoken of here, but is very alive in my heart. While I am forever changed by my experience in Freudian psychoanalysis and consider this the best secular education I have received, I will never forget how loyal my analyst was to Sigmund Freud. I will continue to read psychoanalytic literature and biographies of Freud.

When I heard Joel Whitebook, a philosopher and psycho-analyst, mention on an International Psychoanalytical Association podcast, speculate that Freud had cut off from his early feelings, I felt proud of myself for letting go of the idealization I had created about my perfect early childhood. The six-year period I spent with my mother as an only child no longer appeared idyllic. Granted Mom and I had a lot of fun but my enmeshment with her was not without cost. Because she gave me anything I wanted, I didn't learn to handle disappointment or learn how to share attention. As I was patting myself on the back for honoring this realization, a black-and-white image of me appeared at the age of eighteen, fresh out of high school, being dropped off at college. Initially, the memory wasn't in full Kodachrome color. I needed to develop these memories using all the skills I had acquired from the overlapping of the secular and the sacred.

I asked myself why the memories of this period of my life rose to the surface right now. Was the upcoming separation from the analyst a comparable event? In search of answers, I shut my eyes and pictured how Mom and her mother, the woman I called Little Gram, helped me load up my belongings in a nine-passenger blue 1959 Chevy station wagon with an electric back window switch that my siblings and I fought over to operate. Mom was driving me to Morningside College, the largest United Methodist college in Iowa; Dad was in the cornfield. I had chosen Morningside because it was the farthest from our farm of any of the United Methodist colleges in Iowa. I wanted to enroll in a college sponsored by my church, but one not too close to home so they wouldn't bother me. I wanted to be on my own. My parents let me know without really putting it in words that it was too expensive to drive to the college just to see where I would be. I wasn't surprised at their frugality and didn't mind that we wouldn't be able to scout out my new life ahead of time. I just wanted a new life.

Little Gram insisted that I sit in the front seat by Mom so I could help navigate our way as the three of us had never been to Sioux City, four hours from our farm—a distance that to me felt akin to setting off for a foreign country. When we arrived on campus, it was the first time I had ever set eyes on where I would be spending the next year of my life. I remember Mom being upset that my dorm room in Dimmit Hall on the third floor, which meant a lot of huffing and puffing up the stairs lugging my gear, was so tacky, the paint coming off the walls, the furniture downright shabby.

I thought the room was wonderful—it felt like mine even though I had to share it with a roommate. I wanted Mom and Little Gram to leave as soon as we got my stuff unpacked. I was eager to feel the freedom of being on my own. I wanted my privacy, the privacy psychoanalytical thinking later explained as being intimately involved in developing and stabilizing a sense of self, autonomy, social competence, integration, and freedom of imagination (Schafer, The Reality Principle, Tragic Knots, and the Analytic Process, 2007).

These memories rapidly discharged from my unconscious to my conscious mind. I moved my head up and down as if to indicate yes and blinked my eyes: were these feelings, ones from fifty-seven years ago, feelings I was having about leaving psychoanalysis? During my many years in analysis, I had gained great respect for the unconscious, in particular my unconscious, so I felt certain there was a reason I was thinking about leaving home for college as my planned year of termination was nearing an end.

I hoped these memories had surfaced as encouragement and as a reminder of my first stab at autonomy. That they were there to remind me of how rich and varied my experience had been during my one year of campus living in a girls' dormitory in the days where when a man visited, we yelled,

"Man on the hall!" and of the jealousy I had felt when a female classmate placed a rose and an announcement that she was engaged in the lobby. How certain I was that the only authentic love was married love and how I wanted union sooner, not later. The memories reminded me of how my roommate Sue, and I rode the bus downtown (the first bus beside the yellow school bus I had ever boarded) and how much fun we had as she used her entire year's allowance by the end of October. How generous she had been with me, sharing chocolates, and how angry her father was when she asked for more money.

During my year on campus, I had loved the requirement that all students attend Chapel once a week, which was held in the on-campus United Methodist Church. As a girl, I had been envious when I found out that Catholics were required to attend Mass every day. I wished we had been required to go to chapel every day. Most of my fellow students resented having to attend what was essentially a church service during the week, but I loved the hush that occurred when we were sitting quietly. The prayers for the world were more intense because rather than everyone being the same color as in my rural church, there were people from all over the world sitting in the pews all around me. Even the hymns were inspiring as many of us, especially those of us in chorus, made beautiful harmony. Of course, there were days when I wanted to sleep in and defy the requirement. I was surprised that reminiscing about departure for my year of college happened so spontaneously and that I had been reminded of my spiritual nature.

I suspected that my unconscious was busting through, trying to inform me that it was time for me to leave psychoanalysis—to leave the relationship with the analyst, a relationship practically as important to me as my relationship with my mother. I had discovered so much about myself through my relationship with the analyst and the work we accomplished. It was difficult to imagine not having her in my life. She had taught me, without ever using professional technical words, Freud's reality principle and Freud's pleasure principle. I had read that among the analysand's magical expectations, one became prominent during the termination process: a magical expectation that because of the treatment, all sources of conflict would be eliminated. I nodded my head when I came across what I viewed as a wish for perfection. My tendency to rise above vulnerabilities, pain, and conflicts still remained; however, I knew these habit-patterns had been tempered. My goal now was to experience non-psychotic magic. Magic made possible by my new relationship to reality as it is.

EPILOGUE

Reminiscing on fantasies that accompanied me a decade ago while crossing the threshold into the analyst's office, I realize I was looking for magic. I wanted an all-knowing analyst to not only formulate the questions that needed to be asked but provide answers, if not directly, by hinting at what her choice would be. As the years went by, I discovered the analyst was not a magician but a purveyor of insight, embracing and expressing knowledge connected to a level of thinking that I had previously made a practice of avoiding. As this memoir, a labor of love describing the final year in Freudian psychoanalysis, comes to a close, I pause to acknowledge and pay tribute to the psychological layers I discovered during the termination year. I am happy to report that when beginning the termination year, I was fully aware I was not working with a wizard, but with an experienced psychoanalyst, trained in the intricacies of her trade, eager and willing to meet me in the present moment.

The paradoxical nature of termination from Freudian psychoanalysis becomes evident as I describe termination in terms of an ending but also as a beginning. I do not want to idealize or mythologize the burgeoning sense of agency that emerged as I left analytical treatment. Reentering householder life following the yearlong termination process, I was free from the dyadic structure of Freud's psychoanalytic setting where it was expected I project important relationships from the past onto the analyst. Leaving her, I could now view her not as a judge or god, but as an ordinary human being with specific skills and knowledge of psychoanalysis. A person who knew how to maintain connections despite my stubborn resistance. This new agency was also inspired by my study of the breadth and depth of psychoanalytic theory. My particular fascination with the mind and body connection appeared to be an interest I had in common with Freud. Freud wanted to solve the puzzle of the somatic interaction with the psyche but was unable to because the science of his time didn't have the tools.

Claiming and integrating my inner life put me in touch with a new story, a new narrative that would accompany me through the rest of my life. This revised life story reinserted my sense of the sacred that had been on sabbatical during much of my analytical treatment. A person looking at my life might declare that nothing had changed. That would be an error. Though it might appear that nothing was different, the new sense of responsibility I felt put me in control, without reverting to my habitual above it all position. In more than fourteen years of Freudian psychoanalysis, I had learned to study, contemplate, and integrate what I was ingesting. All of which reconnected me with the seeker I had always been. The part of me that for longer than I wanted to admit had disregarded my inner knowing had learned to pay attention, at last. I began to focus more on impressing myself by activating my new behaviors and less on being concerned what the analyst thought.

I have learned to pay attention to what Freud named the unconscious—thoughts and feelings that are below normal consciousness. As I indicated previously, I came to psychoanalysis seeking magic and found insight. Most strikingly, insight into how my need for the oceanic feeling spoke to my brokenness which then could lead me to transcending the anxiety. Focusing on the sense of unity I craved, I avoided conflict, distrusted my own reality, while deferring to others with stronger opinions. Entering analysis, I was in a transitional period of life, grieving for the breakup of a marriage entered at age eighteen, a marriage I thought would last forever. Entering the termination year, I was also in a transitional period, learning to live with a partner who was there for me in healthy ways.

What is life after psychoanalysis? It consists of the deep sense of strength I often feel and want to always feel but since I am a human being, it is not always present. There are still really hard days, but more days are an even mixture of awe, wonder, and a search for meaning. If I could tell you one thing, it would be to embrace your sense of brokenness and honor it. Jump into your body with its wisdom and ability to be in the now moment. Pay attention to the inner knowing that you try to repress. Taking in Freud's reality principal doesn't have to disenchant the world. Being with this type of reality may bring you to true enlightenment. You have a source of great power inside you alongside the hunger and yearning that keeps you up at night. To stay in the ambivalence is very difficult, but as you learn more about not jumping to opinions on what it right or wrong, good or bad, reality will reveal joy, love, and creativity.

ACKNOWLEDGMENTS

My debut memoir, *Fear, Folly & Freud,* described the personal transformation made possible by over a decade of psychoanalytic treatment. This second memoir focuses more particularly on the spiritual side of this transformation, especially after I decided to bring this chapter of my life to a close. While psychoanalysis and spiritual exploration are both seen primarily as solitary journeys, the truth is that personal growth is not possible without other people.

The following deserve special mention:

Barbara Boyd is an extraordinary book coach who supported me during the writing of my first memoir. Since she always seems to get what I am trying to say and assists me in articulating it, I was overjoyed when she agreed to journey with me again on this project.

My dear friend John Broomfield and I have shared writing and a love of India with each other since 1994! When I mentioned I was looking for a publisher for my next book, he recommended Atmosphere Press, the publisher of his memoir, *Carried on Great Winds.*

Barbara lives in Italy and John in New Zealand, so you can imagine my astonishment when I spoke with Kyle McCord, acquisitions editor for Atmosphere Press, and learned he lives blocks from me in Urbandale. It was exciting to meet with him in person at my home. I appreciate Kyle's straightforward approach and enthusiasm.

Writing takes a great deal of time and energy. Here are a few of the people who have been involved in no less important ways for this memoir to come into being.

Sarah, our personal chef, comes once a week to cook for my husband and me. Not only that, but she also listens attentively to my writing ideas and offers helpful suggestions. She and several of her friends were members of my first writing group.

Sanela's Cleaning Crew cleans our home. These women, originally from Bosnia, burst in the door once a month, energetically asking, "How are you?" before getting started scrubbing and dusting everything.

Special appreciation goes to my three sons:

Matthew helpfully shared his knowledge of the satisfactions, frustrations, and need for persistence, which he remembered as part of writing his doctoral dissertation. Watching as Matt creates a family with his wife, Marcy, and then grows into the role of grandfather has been an unbelievable gift.

Mark surprises me with insightful written comments regarding my weekly posts. He plays the guitar and sings at local venues in San Diego. He is preparing to teach his daughter how to drive in San Diego.

Mason is establishing a home in New Mexico with his sweetheart, Lisbeth. He has been working closely with me to develop a presence on social media and now edits my blog posts with a focus on adding complexity while maintaining a one-pointed focus. I marvel at how deeply he knows the English language and life in general, then remember he is a translator who lived a decade in Brazil.

Wendell, my husband, lovingly picks up my library books and frequently buys flowers to cheer me up. He listens to my frustrations and is always there to solve any problem I present to him. Many times he sets the table, and he always cleans up the kitchen. His dry wit keeps me laughing. I couldn't make it without him.

BIBLIOGRAPHY

Benjamin, J. (2018). *Beyond Doer and Done To*. New York: Routledge.

Bettelheim, B. (1982). *Freud and Man's Soul*. New York: Knopf.

Downing, C. (1977). Re-Visioning Autobiography: The Bequest of Freud and Jung. *Soundings: An Interdisciplinary Journal*, pp. 210-228.

Downing, C. (2005). *Preludes: Essays on the Ludic Imagination, 1961-1981*. Lincoln, NE: iUniverse.

Eigen, M. (2010). *Eigen in Seoul: Volume One, Madness and Murder* (Vol. Volume One). London: Karnac Books Ltd.

Eigen, M. (2011). *Faith and Transformation* (Vol. Eigen in Seoul: Volume Two). London: Karnac.

Freud, S. (1955, 2010). *The Interpretation of Dreams: The Complete and Definitive Text*. (J. Strachey, Ed., & J. Strachey, Trans.) New York: Basic Books.

Frosh, S. (2006). *For and Against Psychoanalysis* (Vol. Second edition). Hove, East Sussex: Routledge.

Gabbard, G. O. (1996). *Love and Hate in The Analytic Setting*.

Northvale, New Jersey: Jason Aronson Inc.

Girgus, S. B. (1990). *Desire and the Political Unconscious in American Literature.* New York: St. Martin's Press.

Hewitt, M. A. (2014). *Freud on Religion.* New York: Foutledge.

Kantrowitz, J. L. (2015). *Myths of Termination:What Patients Can Teach Psychoanalysts About Endings.* New York: Routledge.

Matthews, J. (1991). *The Celtic Shaman: A Handbook.* Boston, MA: Element Books, Inc.

Petrucelli, J. P. (Ed.). (2010). *Knowing, Not-Knowing, & Sort of Knowing.* London: Karnac.

Poland, W. (1996). *Melting the Darkness: The Dyad and Principles of Clinical Practice.* Northvale, NJ: Jason Aronson.

Roiphe, K. (2016). *The Violet Hour: Great Writers at the End.* New York: Penguin Random House, LLC.

Rubin, J. B. (1998). *A Psychoanalysis For Our Time.* New York: New York University Press.

Schafer, R. (1983). *The Analytic Attitude.* New York: Basic Books, Inc.

Schafer, R. (2007). The Reality Principle, Tragic Knots, and the Analytic Process. *Journal of the American Psychoanalytic Association*, Vol. 55, issue 4.

Schwartz, H. (Ed.). (2020). *The Jewish Tought and Psychoanalysis Lectures.* Oxfordshire: Phoenix Publishing House Ltd.

Whitebook, J. (2017). *Freud: An Intellectual Biography.* New York: Cambridge University Press.

ABOUT THE AUTHOR

Nicola Mendenhall, known to her family and friends as Nicky, is a retired psychotherapist. Feeling stymied in her own personal growth, she decided to try Freudian psychoanalysis. A decade later, she found that engaging in four sessions a week had ingrained a habit of self-exploration that she continued in her writing. Ignoring her fear of embarrassment, Nicky chose to document this harrowing psychoanalytic journey, including her fraught relationship with the analyst. She hoped that as others resonated with these experiences, they would engage in some aspect of personal growth. This first memoir, *Fear, Folly & Freud: A Psychotherapist in Psychoanalysis* was published on her seventy-fifth birthday.

Nicky describes issues she struggled with in analysis: anger, intimate relationships, and learning to trust the unconscious.

Because the process of writing sustained and nourished her personal transformation, she now offers writing groups for persons wanting to uncover their genuine selves.

When she's not writing, Nicky loves playing Pepper with friends and family, walking in nature, and reading psychoanalytic literature, other people's memoirs, and exploring the fascinating mind/body connection. A longstanding meditation practice with both the Open Heart Project and Zen Fields helps her mind continue to awaken.

She cherishes relationships with each of her three sons and through her marriage to Wendell Speers in 2009 gained two daughters and their husbands, who are also truly gifts. Altogether, she and Wendell have six grandchildren and one incredibly special great-grandson.

To contact Nicky, visit her website nicolamendenhall.com or email her at nicola.mendenhall@gmail.com.

ABOUT ATMOSPHERE PRESS

Atmosphere Press is an independent, full-service publisher for excellent books in all genres and for all audiences. Learn more about what we do at atmospherepress.com.

We encourage you to check out some of Atmosphere's latest releases, which are available at Amazon.com and via order from your local bookstore:

Finding Us, by Kristin Rehkamp

The Ideological and Political System of Banselism, by Royard Halmonet Vantion (Ancheng Wang)

Unconditional: Loving and Losing an Addict, by Lizzy and Adam

Telling Tales and Sharing Secrets, by Jackie Collins, Diana Kinared, and Sally Showalter

Nursing Homes: A Missionary's Journey Through Heaven's Waiting Room, by Tim Eatman Ph.D.

Timeline of Stars, by Joe Adcock

A Boy Who Loved Me, by Wilson Semitti

The Injustice in Justice, by Charmaine Loverin

Living in the Gray, by Katie Weber

Living with Veracity, Dying with Dignity, by Alison Clay-Duboff

Noah's Rejects, by Rob Kagan

A lot of Questions (with no answers)?, by Jordan Neben

Cowboy from Prague: An Immigrant's Pursuit of the American Dream, by Charles Ota Heller

Sleeping Under the Bridge, by Melissa Baker

The Only Prayer I Ever Have to Say Is Thank You, by M. Kaya Hill

Amygdala Blue, by Paul Lomax

www.ingramcontent.com/pod-product-compliance
Lightning Source LLC
Chambersburg PA
CBHW032035050726
47590CB00006B/2412